Life List

"The poems in *Life List* offer an extraordinary depiction of life from childhood through old age, moving us to tears and laughter through reminiscence, dreams, and evocations of classical and contemporary art and letters."

—**Bonnie Braendlin**, author of the Caulfield, Sheridan Mystery Series

"McCann is a religious poet, but not in a pedestrian or fundamentalist sense. From Italy to Texas, these poems deal with nostalgia. How to retrieve 'it'—if not now, then at some future point. How to please get it back. From a deceased husband's memory to fleeing from the pandemic. From a crummy bar in Florence or a lost painting, we must go on, and we do.

—**Sybil Estess**, author of *Mississippi Milkwater*

"How do I love the poetry of Janet McCann? Let me count the ways: her wicked sense of humor, her clear eye, her choice of organizing this book around growing up and growing old in mid-century America, and her refusal to give in to despair, though loss is all around. I loved every single poem in this collection, and you, dear reader, will too."

—**Barbara Crooker**, author of *The Book of Kells*

"McCann's volume of new and selected poems, *Life List*, begins by taking readers on a trip to an almost-forgotten world of a childhood seventy years ago. The first poems reference such memory ticklers as bathing caps, jelly glasses, a child slung over a parent's shoulder being called 'a sack of potatoes,' and the bright wax lips that were sold in candy stores as a Halloween disguise. We watch as the child of the early poems matures and steps out into the world with ever an eye toward the tactile, the contradictory, the urgent, and the ordinary, all of which she has recorded and generously shares with her readers. Later poems look back with new insight and appreciation for the life she has lived. The book is an invitation to each reader to give thought to his or her life through the prism of the author's reflections on her own."

—**Christine H. Boldt**, author of *For Every Tatter*

Life List

New and Selected Poems

Janet Lacey McCann

RESOURCE *Publications* · Eugene, Oregon

LIFE LIST
New and Selected Poems

Copyright © 2021 Janet Lacey McCann. All rights reserved. Except for brief quotations in critical publications or reviews, no part of this book may be reproduced in any manner without prior written permission from the publisher. Write: Permissions, Wipf and Stock Publishers, 199 W. 8th Ave., Suite 3, Eugene, OR 97401.

Resource Publications
An Imprint of Wipf and Stock Publishers
199 W. 8th Ave., Suite 3
Eugene, OR 97401

www.wipfandstock.com

PAPERBACK ISBN: 978-1-6667-0484-6
HARDCOVER ISBN: 978-1-6667-0485-3
EBOOK ISBN: 978-1-6667-0486-0

AUGUST 24, 2021

For all my family, in this life and the next

ACKNOWLEDGMENTS

I WOULD LIKE TO thank the journals in which some of these poems first appeared: *America, Atlanta Review, Birmingham Poetry Review, Bloodroot, Blue Unicorn, Bryant Literary Review, Christian Century, Descant, Forum, Common Grounds Review, Connecticut River Review, Green Mountains Review, Hospital Drive, Illya's Honey, Midwest Quarterly, New Laurel Review, Mudfish, Midwest Quarterly, Permafrost, Pivot, Poet, Poet and Critic, Puerto del Sol, Rattle, Sou'wester, Texas Poetry Calendar, Texas Review, Texas Slough, Valparaiso Poetry Review, U.S. Catholic,* and *Weber Studies*

Contents

ACKNOWLEDGMENTS | vii

DAYBREAK

FIRST MEMORY | 3
DIALOGUE WITH THE DOGCATCHER | 4
1947 | 8
ROADS TO EVERYWHERE | 9
TUMBLERS | 10
MAP TEST | 11
SOUL SLEEP | 13
WHAT SHE CRAVES | 15
DEPARTMENT STORES OF CHILDHOOD | 16
TWO TATTERED PIANO BOOKS | 17
FIRST TRIP | 19
CARTWHEELS, WE | 21
THE WASHING MACHINE | 22
KINDERGARTEN FAITH | 23
DR. M | 24
HALLOWEEN CARNIVAL, 1948 | 25
A PRESBYTERIAN CHILD TAKES PIANO LESSONS AT THE CONVENT OF THE SACRED HEART, 1949 | 27

DOUBLE EXPOSURE, 1940 | 29
KATY KEENE | 30
AROUND THE FIRE | 31
QUICK, WHAT HAS VANISHED? | 32
GHOSTS OF CHRISTMAS | 33

MORNING

HOW GOOD IT WOULD BE | 37
CHILD WITH A BOOK | 38
VIGILANTES | 40
LOT'S WIFE | 41
AIOLI | 42
THE TRIP | 43
THE HELIUM BALLOON | 44
ON THE ROOF | 45
LOOKING AT THE CHRISTMAS PHOTOS | 46
THE NARRATIVE HOUSE | 47
FROM, RECEIVED BY, ACTED UPON, IN TIME | 49
VICKI'S SOUP | 52
CHATEAU D'EAU | 54
I AM NO GARDENER | 56
DURING THE MUSEUM TOUR | 57
LA BELLE ANGÈLE (1889) | 58
HERE | 60
GIRL MAKING A GARLAND (@1480) | 63
FRA ANGELICO'S 'THE ANNUNCIATION' (@ 1448) | 64
THE ORCHARD | 65
ITALIAN NOCTURNE | 67
THE HOME OF THE RADIOACTIVE CATS (1980) | 68

NASTURTIUMS | 69

EDVARD MUNCH | 70

FLOW | 71

LUM'S POND | 72

from ORDINARY SAINTS | 74

SAM'S | 77

WATERPOEM | 78

EXPLANATION | 79

THE RED SWEATER IN THE SMITHSONIAN | 80

HEINZ CHAPEL | 81

FLOWERING CACTUS | 82

PHYSICS | 83

NOON

ANSWERING MACHINE | 87

LOST IN THE ZOO OF TO BE | 88

PASCAL AT THE RACES | 89

THE NURSERYMAN | 92

READING THE CIRCULAR | 93

KLIMT'S GARDEN | 94

FORBIDDEN IMAGES | 95

HOTEL | 96

AFTERNOON

FRONTIER | 99

TRANSLATION EXERCISE | 100

REDEMPTION | 102

SHOP WINDOW: THE FASHION IN BRUSSELS | 104

I DON'T | 107

PEELING | 108

xi

NINETEEN THIRTY-SIX | 109
MY FATHER'S HOUSE | 125
THE SPIDERS OF CHERNOBYL | 132

EVENING

REPORT TO THE ASSESSOR-COLLECTOR | 137
SIX AND A HALF WAYS OF LOOKING AT A CAT | 138
THE THREE AGES OF EUROPE | 140
EXTRACTIONS | 141
THE CRONE AT THE CATHOLIC CONFERENCE | 142
ON THE GROUNDS OF THE MONASTERY WHERE FRA ANGELICO PAINTED | 143
GALILEO'S EYE | 144
OLD CINDERELLA | 147
SYLVIA AT SIXTY | 148
THE CRONE AT THE CATHEDRAL | 149
LAUNDRY | 150
THE BOOKSTORE ON BROADWAY IN ALBANY: AWP CONFERENCE 1999 | 151
THE AUTUMN NAME OF GOD | 152
CASTIGLION FIORENTINO SATURDAY | 153
MOVEMENT, SOLITUDE, SPACE | 154
AT THE LIENDO | 156
SLEEPING WOMEN IN MOVIES | 157
THE CAT AT THE END OF THAT POETRY ANTHOLOGY | 158
MONASTERY CATS | 159
IN ANOTHER BAR | 160
IN THE ALZHEIMER'S WARD | 161
THE CRONE AT THE AUSTIN POETRY FESTIVAL | 163

OLD FRIENDSHIP | 165

THE GALLERY OF LOST ART | 167

from WIDOWING | 169

TRIAGE | 173

QUESTION POSED BY A PAINTING OF
   SAVONAROLA | 174

MEMORY LANE | 176

IN DREAMS | 178

THE CRONE RESPONDS TO A POEM ON VERSE DAILY
   WHICH COMPLAINS ABOUT USELESS POETRY THAT
   DOES NOT ADDRESS INJUSTICE | 179

GUILT | 180

CROSSWORD | 182

IN THE FRONT GARDEN | 183

WALKERS OF THE SEEN AND UNSEEN | 184

75TH 4TH | 185

CORONA | 186

CORONA BOREDOM | 187

ORDINARY TIME | 188

HOUSES | 189

MY GRANDDAUGHTER POSTPONES HER WEDDING
   BECAUSE OF THE PANDEMIC | 193

LIFE LIST | 194

NIGHT

About the author | 197

DAYBREAK

"The events of childhood do not pass but repeat themselves like seasons of the year."

—Eleanor Farjeon

"Children are like wet cement. Whatever falls on them makes an impression."

—Dr. Hiam Ginnot

FIRST MEMORY

I am not yet two.
brick wall, grass,
my mother: g*ive Patty the cup,*
you have to learn to share

the bright grass, the dark red of the bricks
if I go further I think I make things up
Patty a brunette
and now I'm seeing a sandbox

I'm close to 80 now
how can I sort remember from invent
next scene we have been playing leapfrog
—but I remember or I remember remembering

A plastic cup the word *share*
some small door opening
a tiny hand reaching out into the universe
offering a cup of light

DIALOGUE WITH THE DOGCATCHER

(for Paul, who did not become a dogcatcher)

I say son
lets talk about this D
you start getting Ds in third grade
and youll never get into college.

he says
its okay mom
Im not going.
Im going to be the dogcatcher.

I look at him
ready to get mad
but hes serious.
you dont have to go to college
to be the dogcatcher he says
just high school
but Id really like to
start now.

nobody wants to be
the dogcatcher I say
its a terrible job.
you chase dogs
and pen them up
if the owners dont come
you take the dogs out
and shoot them.

not me he says
the dogs Im spose to shoot
Ill just take home
to this old house Ill buy
out in the country
for the dogs and me.

thats why Im going to be
the dogcatcher.

you cant do that I say
even if theres not
some law against it.
youll catch sick dogs
and hurt ones.
youll have to shoot them.

Ill heal them he says.

to do that I say
you have to be a vet.
to go to vet school
you need all As.

these will be dogs
no one cares about he says.
they wont know if the person
who heals them
is a vet or not.

well anyway I say
you cant be getting Ds
and we spend the next half hour
doing multiplication tables.

I find out I dont know anymore
what 6 X 12 is
and he goes to bed.

that night in my dream
he stops for me
in an old blue pickup.
his report card
is pinned over the inside mirror
framed in gold.
it has an official seal on it
the D stands for dogcatcher.
hes maybe forty
wearing a sleazy jacket
with the elbows worn thin.
hes a little overweight
but has the same smile.
his front seat is littered
with beer cans
and milkbones.
what happened to your good suit
I say.
he drives me to his place
which turns out to be
a ruined plantation
by the Mississippi.
first I see the roof
through the foliage
then the whole house.
its a massive wreck
gone all to goldenrod
half the walls missing
hundreds of rooms
exposed to air
fluted column broken
spiral staircase leading

up to nowhere

and all these dogs!
mutts and borzois
dachshunds dobermans
basenjis shepherds
retrievers even a halfwolf
poking around in the vines

dogs in all the rooms
on the stairs
and around the house.

my god I say.

they look up at him
and thousands of tails wag.

I have all the dogs here
that no one wants he says
but I have to keep at it.
every few minutes
somebody throws one away
dumps it along a highway
or in someone elses garden.
its not an easy job
being the dogcatcher.

dawn light wakes me
to the narrow room,
textbook lying in dust.

1947

She asks why am I
me, the hum of summer rising
from all the hedges,

the why like bubbles
coming to the surface of her body
prickling her skin.

Her name is in the clouds,
in sidewalk cracks
spelled out in the field
with leaves and twigs.

Smell of moss, dew
drying off the grass,
her regulation bathing cap
flapping on her arm
down the path to the pool.

She asks, why not
anyone else, the sun beats
down on her unmarked skin,
her strange isolation of self

which suddenly seems to rise
out of her, evaporate.
Light passes through her.

ROADS TO EVERYWHERE

In the first grade they gave me *Roads to Everywhere*
instead of Dick and Jane. I missed my turn
because I was following those roads, going everywhere.
The town was one square mile. On all four sides
a road led out of it, but I never took them.
Saturdays were the park. I whirled and whirled
on the playground merry-go-round, lay dizzy in the sand
and watched the sky spin by. Sundays
the big stone church, O *Rock of Ages*, ice-cream
in a neighbor's yard, or at grandmother's house,
three streets over on Main Street. I know still
that old address: 244 Main, though for thirty years
there's been no house there. CH4 2443.
"Number please," the operator said
when I lifted the black spindle. I did this often
until the operator called grandmother,
told her to make me stop. The busy signal
a frightening dark electric noise. Crossing the street
was not allowed, although I saw maybe
ten cars drive down it daily. Over on Main —
scissors-grinders, tinkers, salesmen of fruits and
vegetables, the teenaged sausage vendor
whose wares were most forbidden, whose bicycle I chased
down the street with a dime, usually couldn't catch him,
watched the battered bike go out of town
toward Everywhere. Caught up once—
his chain had broken—ate the greasy sausage
behind the garage. These years were the forties
which we inhabited with careful blindness,
the war a fuzzy noise on the radio,
somewhere even the west road would never take me.

TUMBLERS

In all the old movies, cut or pressed glass,
men with scotch or bourbon in them.
I have six, they were my father's glasses.

Don pours himself a scotch in the office.
Men, doing business, smiling, clinking, talking.
I run my fingers over the bumpy surface,

implied flowers, triangles, prisms.
I always knew where Dad was in the house
by the tinkle of ice. I'd track him down,

but he would never share the golden fluid,
told me stories he said he'd read in the *Detroit
Free Press,* about me, though my name

was a little different, I was Joanette Loesey.
When the glass was empty he took more.
Sometimes he said he felt sick, and let me fix

an Alka-Seltzer. That he shared.
Bitter, sour, chemical and bubbly.
It was delicious.

MAP TEST

Points on a map, I never knew them,
which was Cincinnati, which Columbus.
State by state. Rivers and towns and cities.
Blue ditto marks on fragile yellow paper.
A drop of ink widened to a dime,
drowning several cities. North Dakota,
was it on top of South? That thick blue line,
was it the Mississippi, or just a state
boundary? I squinted, looked at Ardeth's
paper, but she didn't know them either.

The whole geography, the world beyond the town
a letter in an unknown language, not of interest
beyond a grade, rivers a blue squiggle,
coastlines likewise, some crosshatchings
to indicate the sea, the gulf, the bay?
After school we went to the gas station
to buy wax lips. We pressed them gently
to each other's cheeks, then chewed them
to a red blob. —*Where will you live
when you grow up?* —*New York, of course,*

which gave 5% on the test, later I learned
Chicago. Now in age I love them,
the maps, keep them for distant countries,
for every state I've ever driven through,
folded maps, Trip-Tiks, guidebooks,
pages from Mapquest. What a thrill
to find out that the place is where the page said!

They indicate design, the feeling when
starting off, that surely the road must end
somewhere on the map where you want to go.

SOUL SLEEP

Psychopannychy: The state in which (according to some) the soul
sleeps between death and the day of judgment." OED

at the universe's edge, the county of Zeno
tossing and turning of souls
on the bumpy infinite mattress

as after death the long hand still rolls round
calendar pages drift
into your ghostly sleep

forms and faces rise
"we will reserve judgment"
what dreams we have   when once

light dwindles under lids
flickers of leached colors
scrawled palimpsests, scatter of dying sparks

picture forming outline sharpening
under the chemical bath
to awaken

and the cold filters through darkness
soullimbs drawn in
a garment of lawn tossed over

two-dimensional figures converse without consonants
nothing to desire or fear
no desire

but in the space where it was
the burnt-out quasar of love,
drop of water tearlike

on the quick sharp pinpoint of time

WHAT SHE CRAVES

She hungers for mystery,
      fortuitous connections, hints
that there is something beyond not only
            her comprehension but anyone's.

She wants an animal living behind her house
      that has no fellow, he is the only one.
           She looks for his track, his leavings.
      Imagines dark fur, intelligent eyes.

We all have our own secrets, and they make us
      all the more desirable.

Without them, we are jelly glasses on a shelf,
    for use in emergencies but offering
            neither beauty nor promise.

These books I read in Italian
      are wonderful because I only partly
         understand them,

So I receive with gladness
            Emily's gift of flowers
              and cryptic lines
    sent to Sue maybe 150 years ago, she put

the flowers in a vase, but left
          the mystery in the lines.

DEPARTMENT STORES OF CHILDHOOD

Magic rooms with shelves of everything
    I could even think of wanting.
And separated, too. There were *departments*.
        Now at night
Angelic forms announce the floors. Hardware and dreams
On twelve. Dogs and fish on three.
On eleven, Cabbage Patch dolls, pens and incense.
Witch balls in the basement, with medicines
And alchemy equipment. There are escalators
    Also but they are too steep.

Package-laden, I will have tea
With my grandmother on the roof:
    A three tiered tray with fairy cakes and scones.
The bus home stops at the front door.

TWO TATTERED PIANO BOOKS

1

The writing has faded
Next to the tarnished stars
On lessons I stumbled through
Seventy years ago in a front parlor

While behind glass doors
A grandfather clock ticked
And an old husband rocked
Amidst disordered cushions

Never wincing at sour notes
Puffing at his pipe,
He never looked up
From his *Saturday Evening Post*

At me or my jolly teacher,
Round Mrs. Ellery
Who chortled now and then, "You rascal,
You really ought to practice more"

And played a merry treble trill
To mark the end of the lesson.

2

No stars on this memento
Of angular, angry Miss Emerson
Who held the ruler ready
To chastise errant fingers

Who watched and listened frowning
As I arranged the silences
As one by one the dead notes fell
Under the bronze bust of Schubert.

Here it is: dim room
A papery smell, dying flowers
My awkward fingers moving
Over the black and white keys

While outside booms
The joyous, discordant afternoon.

FIRST TRIP

A bus. I was three. Chatham to
Morristown, to my grandmother's genteel
shop, The Knitting Lounge.

The great machine, pictures on the walls,
maps. Straight down Main Street
that turned into Madison Avenue

and went right past my house. I held
grandmother's hand at the bus stop under the picture
that said BUS. I knew the word.

On the sign a shadow grownup
held hands with a shadow child. I was going
away. Mother was upset, but I had to go,

there was some emergency. As we boarded
grandmother dropped a dime, I found it,
gave it to the driver. "Newark,"

I said proudly. The Lounge bored me to
tears, screams actually, I had to be pacified
with a box of Hall's Cough Drops,

and a woman who was there knitting booties
gave me cookies I was not allowed to eat,
and when I got home my behavior was

a cause for grave concern. But how I loved
the great metal box that took us all
to Morristown. I dreamed of it

for years, sitting in the driver's seat
calling off the stops, swerving left, right,
my feet not touching the floor.

CARTWHEELS, WE

could do them once, though
awkwardly, the quick body
thrust & swing & the being
upside down, world revolving
& sky swinging underneath
& then there we were,
standing upright and sudden
looking across the lawn;

this was the closest thing
to those dreams of lying
where it was no surprise
to find ourselves aloft,
the skill we needed in secret
muscles under our shoulder-
blades, exercised only
at night amid the flowers
grown wild & bright
in our translated yard.

THE WASHING MACHINE

The new washing machine, it is
something to praise,

with its swirl of suds and shirts,
its whooshes and thumps

that harmonize with my reading.
I did once wash my clothes in the stream,

shook the sparkling drops out,
hung shirts on the line without even wringing.

I did not think or worry where the suds
went, carried downstream, but then

this was no detergent, Mémé made the soap,
I don't know how. In the afternoon

I'd fold the clothes and lay them in the basket,
carry it back to the house light as my breath,

wooden handles bobbing in my grip
and singing the song of the river . . .

KINDERGARTEN FAITH

I colored the outlined Christ the Shepherd—
black crook, brown cloak, brown sandals.
But I added the sheep on my own.
They were like clouds, clouds with eyes.
Picasso eyes, I would say now.
Some were happy, some puzzled.
I blamed my lack of skill.
But they have to have eyes, I said.

My sheep drifted into the margins,
one even went over the edge of the
page, onto the table. I finished him
because he seemed to want it.
The woman with the Crayola box
was angry. The last sheep looked
at me drunkenly from the table top.
I was scolded but I wasn't punished.

I have always had this kind of trouble
with faith, and I can only hope
for mercy rather than justice,
the lumpy rogue sheep
scooped back into the fold.

DR. M

He brought a briefcase full of vials and powders,
tongue depressors, pills, lollipops.
The orange lozenges were sulfa pills.
He counted them out into a paper cup.

He gave us shots sometimes at garden parties,
a swift sting in the upper arm, then candy.
His Doctor license plate let him speed.
My dad was envious but admiring.

He said no swimming when there was polio.
We grumped but did not swim. A doctor said it.
Our families vacationed together in Florida,
the children reluctant friends. We played careful

Parcheesi and Go Fish. Dr. M
did not play, but sat and watched. I remember
the bristly white circle around his pate,
his pale, lined face, the quiet of his hands.

HALLOWEEN CARNIVAL, 1948

That Halloween carnival at Trinity Church
in the thunderstorm, a mere handful of children
dashing from room to room, the tired members
of the Ladies' Guild
    playing their parts as the lightning
flashed in the arched windows—

in the basement, squirtguns aimed at vestry candles,
   three squirts for a quarter,
smoke rising from the extinguished wicks,
   and something was leaking, water ran down the wall.

Take any prize you want, holding hands,
two girls, one boy, two boys, one girl, laughing,

throw the beanbag through the clown's
   red smile—
crack of thunder
   a greater crack, the elm hit, but we
were kites, soaring—

why they didn't fold it up and send us home—
why they didn't lead us into the sanctuary
   to pray,
to wait for parents there with the mild-eyed saints—

but the lightning flashed and the thunder crashed
and we played, played against the growling sky,
the grownups were ours, with the
   witch-painted faces,
the high vaulted windows, the dusty workrooms,

    the friendly dead and their graves,
        the wrought-iron fence of the churchyard—

with what joy we romped through
what had been an alien kingdom,
formality gone,
no lines, and anything you want.

A PRESBYTERIAN CHILD TAKES PIANO LESSONS AT THE CONVENT OF THE SACRED HEART, 1949

My stubby fingers can not make an octave,
no miracles there. I frown and frown
at the metronome, it will not go away.

I steal forbidden glances at black habits
dancing on clotheslines. No underwear:
do they wear any? Above my head

St. Sebastian, pierced, seems to suffer
most from my janglings. The longest hour.
She tries for kindness, hides her disappointment

but not well. I would rather say Hail Marys
than practice, my friend Theresa taught me.
Taking my short-cut through the cemetery

Home. No star today! I scan the names
on stones: Sister Mary Philomena,
Sister Agnes Felicity, Sister Mary

Bartholomew, beneath them the lost names
they had when they were girls. My steps
quicken, are they there, the long-dead sisters,

ghosts of Catherine O'Reilly, Mary Murphy,
half-child, half-nun, laughing across the graveyard?
Shadows fly over me, my chilled hands

clench and unclench in my jacket pockets
as I run breathless toward the open gate.
The raucous crows revile me from the oaks.

DOUBLE EXPOSURE, 1940

My grandfather stands
in the bright snowy street, holding
a bottle of milk, he has
a morning look, glint
in his eye at the sun. (Who taught me
to look at the sun and sneeze.) Quiet man,
carrying his grandchild down the street
like "a sack of kartoffeln." Stowaway
from Austria at fourteen, he never
looked back. What it must have been
in the dark hold, among the potato sacks
in 1900! That was not recorded.
But here he has, it seems, a woman
in his stomach. Blond hair, pearls,
high neckline, not Grandmother
and no one I remember. On Elm Street
in Chatham, New Jersey, between frame houses,
fanlight to the left, shadows of elms
falling across the walk. The beautiful
forgotten face a perfect cameo
beneath his watch chain. Behind him
among the trees are ghosts of other trees,
their branches faintest tracings on the sky.

KATY KEENE

Slim darkhaired cartoon pre-TV heroine
dressed in black decolleté for the
opera, a trim navy suit for the boardroom,
how we loved you! Outside yawned the fifties,

our choices few, marry or perhaps teach
kindergarten. Each frame of you was perfect,
your gloved hand touching a shoulder,
the shirrings and billows of your ball gown.

Page bottom: this outfit was suggested
by Ellen Lyle of Poughkeepsie, New York,
aged nine. Lucky Ellen, how we wished
to see our own names there! All summer long

under the wheezing fan we drew your outfits,
Mary Ann and I, bathing suits for Monaco,
jewels for Inaugurations. Our stocking seams
would be straight as yours someday, princes gaze

discreetly at our ankles. Katy of New York,
Katy of Paris, Boston, always welcomed;
now the band is playing, "Katy, Katy,"
Now a diplomat bends to kiss your hand.

Sometimes you still turn up in dreams, a Katy
blurred into a Mary-Ann-Grown-Up,
waving in elegance and graceful leisure,
sunlight on fabrics, on the whitewashed decks,
a neat salute, aristocrat's farewell
as the yacht heads out toward the darker waters.

AROUND THE FIRE

Around the fire we sing Girl Scout songs.
Tonight is magical,
we can lift Sue Ellen, the heaviest of us, on our fingers.
Logs crackle, a spark jumps forth and
lands on my forearm. I don't care,
I'm proud of my tiny wound.
The grown-ups are 18. They are mysterious and complete.
Someone comes at me with a tube of oily goo.
The fire pops and snaps, the night presses in.
"Peace, I ask of thee, O River," we sing.
I gaze at my arm, white in the wavery light.
I have been bitten by a star.

QUICK, WHAT HAS VANISHED?

(for Stephanie)

Washing dishes next to someone,
Shaking the clear rinse water from spoons and
Passing them along to the one who dries.

Passing them with secrets, sorrows, confessions,
Misunderstandings explained away.

And drying the plates, wiping both sides
With dishcloths illustrated with French spices,
Setting them in a pile, white and gleaming.

Twice a day, breakfast being
Wash-your-own-bowl. The sudsy gray
Wash-basin, the blue rinse-basin.

The chip on the side of the sink.
The slippery bottle of Joy.

GHOSTS OF CHRISTMAS

"If it doesn't happen, you have to do it."
The year I was thirteen was the first time
Christmas wasn't there anymore, and so I rode
my bicycle under the giant candy canes
and Santas, under the pine-decked poles,
their wires hung with lights, looking: I saw
my images flash past in the bright windows as
people with their packages glanced up at this
sort-of-child who wasn't shopping or anything,
just riding around town. Later in dream
I work for the city, hanging shiny globes
on the poles. I work in the hours before
dawn, hanging the globes one by one, a strange
glimmer coming from as they lie
piled in the back of my pickup: and coming to
the edge of town, the tattered edge, everyone
asleep, I hand the last ball and suddenly see
the next town, just on down the road,
hung with those globes, and the next,
and the next, all the sleeping towns,
a magic electric Christmas throughout America.

MORNING

"Given another shot at life, I would seize every minute of it . . . look at it and really see it . . . try it on . . . live it . . . exhaust it . . . and never give that minute back until there was nothing left of it."

—Erma Bombeck

Contemplating childhood is like contemplating a beautiful region as one rides backwards; one really becomes aware of the beauty at that moment, that very instant, when it begins to vanish.

—Soren Kierkegaard

HOW GOOD IT WOULD BE

How good to be under a raggedy quilt
surrounded by dogs, half-asleep,
with soft pillows and the kind of book
you keep reading though it isn't exciting
but the characters are nice, doing their best
through hundreds of chapters. . .
The story goes on in your sleep, the long
Victorian picnic, the wide skirts
like parachutes along the river. Oh
if the world were all comfort, nothing hurting.
I am eating sweet potatoes with walnuts
and butter, now and then a nose
pokes curiously, but the dogs don't care
for the dish enough to disturb me.
If there were just comfort, no pain no challenge,
just soothing sounds, dogs breathing,
cars passing down a gravel road,
a distant train. If I never
had to get up, pay bills, be shouted at
on the telephone, see doctors and
dentists. If nobody ever died.
Could I live in the Comfort world
forever? I knew a woman named
Comfort, she was a Spanish teacher
and taught me sleepy Spanish words,
sueño, ojos cerrados, flotación,
paz, olvido. Her voice was a well
we traveled down, not toward anything,
just away. If she were here.
If Comfort were here now, singing a Spanish song.

CHILD WITH A BOOK
for Olympia

She is edgy and bored in the adult
company. Words go on too long,
words she understands but which do not
connect and have nothing to do with her,
sitting on the edge of the chair
waiting to leave.
Why not try this,
one of the strangers says, and hands her
a book. A disused lamp is lit,
and she leans into the circle of its glow.
Her feet move up, comfortable now,
and the people are all gone with the first
sentence: the tall woman with vague
eyes who handed her the book,
the red-faced men who believe they
are both right. And there she is,
completely in the circle of the lamp
with the good Lion who will die
but not forever and the silly boy
who will learn, but not yet, and they say
important things in the same words
the grown-ups use but these are now
her own, her landscape and her language.

Her long dark hair falls over her still face
and she brushes it back like a curtain,
and when they finally say, it's time
to go, you can finish it later,

it is like coming back through the secret
door into the room where they look for coats
and wraps, and, riding home, eyes shut
as the streetlights flash by, she sees
the lion moving behind heaven's bright bars.

VIGILANTES

You read about them, perfect arbiters
of justice, seeing beyond us
into the depths of evil, cutting it out.
You want a ten-foot tall man or woman
to look into hearts, see what is there.
But they can't be human, because
they might make mistakes. And then
there are always the grey fields, where evil
is not bad enough to smite, but it is there,
corroding. And do they think about
the source of evil, those avengers,
over generations? Or is it just
the black spot, to be cauterized
so the good, even the tepidly good,
can breathe? Who are the good
anyway? Why is ordinary justice
such a lumbering, bumbling machine?
And we still want the avengers we find in books.
And now it is 4 a.m., past the point
of no return on sleep. Thrones
and dominions, principalities and powers.
The infinite pounding of God
on the stone of my heart.

LOT'S WIFE

To look back once
compelled, not by choice,
at the home, self, flaming, verloren,
and then to have the salt come
burning in the throat
congealing the words, the cry
blanked and falling like a stone,

to reach out arms
and have them freeze
to the lost curve of the past—

body and soul
melded in grief
the statue of no!

a receding whiteness
a zero roundness of the lips

AIOLI

The mortar and pestle
must have at least two
generations of use,
garlic worked into the
marble, so that even scrubbed
with pumice, there is a
scent. Use oil from your own
olives, from the trees
behind your house that you
harvested last year. Pound
fresh garlic and tell
your grandmother's stories
of horseback days and lavender nights,
how the chateau
was forbidden to young girls
because of the danger of pregnancy.
Pound and pound, never look
at the clock, which has stopped
years ago anyway. There are no
measurements, the hand
remembers. the yellow sauce
brighter than your tile roof
into which we will dip salt fish
and the vegetables from your garden.

THE TRIP

She asks, "Are we almost there?"
as though we had not just left,
as though the sleeping towns we pass
are milestones, lines on a ruler,
destinations precise as departures.
As the neon eyes blink at her Bill's
Place, Sam's Lunch, Beer, and the
other cars slide down the darkness
in silence, she believes that
we are all going someplace!
How can we tell her, half asleep
under the stars and flashing lights,
that we three are on a möbius trip,
that we somehow slipped through
there at the center where all the
lines of the cloverleaf meet
and we're gliding along the
undersides of highways, always
leaving behind the places where
we never arrived?

THE HELIUM BALLOON

for Jones

It got away
because you wanted it to,
dwindled to a blue point
   beside the sun, went out.
You said where did it go,
   your question a comment,
but I had to answer
   it's hot up there, gases
expand and contract, balloons pop,
   feathery bits of rubber
fall into the sea,
   but believers never listen,
anyway, you didn't really ask,
   and even now a great blue disk
rises over Russia like the moon.

ON THE ROOF

for Paul

diminished neighbors
rake leaves and chat,
smoke of their autumns
drifts beneath me.

here on this blank
asbestos slope
sun-stunned and cautious
I inch toward a peak

where it is always summer,
the line of white
hardening against the sky.
is that your shadow

there on the ridge
or is it only the light
burning the filaments black
as I grope the sun

for the tiny red dot
of the lost plane?

LOOKING AT THE CHRISTMAS PHOTOS

A Pantoum for Peter

We got them back so quickly; here you are
Opening the present. It is red,
It echoes the tree lights. A red plane.
Two days later and the wing is broken.

Opening the present, it is red.
The tree looks just the same. Or does it really?
Two days later and the wing is broken,
It seems brighter and fresher in the picture.

The tree looks just the same. Or does it really?
You sit in the same place, swinging your legs.
It seems brighter and fresher in the picture.
Next week we'll take the bald tree to the dump.

You sit in the same place, swinging your legs;
It echoes the tree lights. A red plane.
Next week we'll take the bald tree to the dump.
We got them back so quickly. Here you are:

THE NARRATIVE HOUSE

"I dwell in Possibility—
A fairer House than Prose—"

Emily Dickinson

the narrator draws the curtains,
    a fine line glides from the pen's bright tip
over the measured blank. they drift now
        in the invisible currents, a mesh more fine
than possibility. the door is drawn shut.
    the room is wet and shimmery and new,
wrapped in its caul of dawn. the narrator frowns:

the picket fence or iron gate? but this
    is the past, so columbine
twines around the scrollwork, everything is there
        to be deciphered. the cemetery
over to the right, or is that too
        obvious? as for the clouds, should they suggest—
no, nothing should lead in any one direction.

but back to the room.   that is perfect now,
    the motes float in this liquid heavier than air
but lighter than water.   now the sound begins.

and this is the road by which the tenants come,
    their boots thumping on the bald cement,

and this is the north end of their coming,
    across the slashed and angled light.

FROM, RECEIVED BY, ACTED UPON, IN TIME
a text and meditation

THE MEDITATION:

Eleanor H Smith, in 1842,
writes most delicately to her beloved
her desire to be removed from where she is.

she has had such a good time, yes, among polite
but perhaps secretly scornful acquaintances,
and she needs the recognition of her place,

the fiancée of, the wife-to-be of,
beginning her letter coyly chastising
her dearest and most beloved

for not writing sooner, scarcely daring
to say what she means: *come get me, come now,*
but gathering courage, as her writing grows

stronger, larger, to ask
maybe even to insist, in 1842,
sending the letter off at twelve and one half cents

(two good restaurant meals? A night in a hotel?)
from Barnstable, Mass to Pawtuckett, RI
—and he must have come, must have brought her back,

else who would have kept this letter
which I have now, its brown paper crumbling
on my desk, in College Station, Texas,
on December 5, 1994,

in this sullen year of Our Lord
(wind in the south, rain coming).

***

The letters of the literary:
a way of missing the meeting,
a chatty absence. Kafka, Proust,
shielding themselves from the dangerous
earthy embrace. Kafka: "The other day
when you wanted me to say I love you,
I had felt compelled to put the answer

in the letter that crossed yours that night
somewhere between here and Berlin;
but perhaps it was obvious anyway
from the opening words of my very
first letter..." and the letters
made whispery papery love, while he
and his Felice did not. And then Proust,
whose letters undermined appointments,
left him wrapped in the quilts of his illness:
"If you decide to come, don't write again,
send a telegram to say you are coming
immediately, and if possible by a train
arriving around ten o'clock in the evening
or in the late afternoon, or after dinner,
but not too late and not before two o'clock...
I am explaining all this in case you come,
but I hope that you will agree with my opinion..."
The guest, of course, did not arrive, and Proust
took his tea alone, the servant dismissed,
vague disappointment and profound relief.

To invent, to construct one's friends and lovers,
to keep them safe in words, never to drop
the pretty painted screen and look,

be looked at, touch—instead to think dimly
of other readers, thousands of faces behind
a fence, like the commoners in the medieval
paintings of Church and State, your face, my face
among them, (I see you, Franz! I see you, Marcel!)
The intimate public thoughts set down, the pen
put decorously aside, the careful folds, the seal.
But Eleanor's world was real.

THE TEXT:

Barnstable, August 8th 1842

My dearest and most beloved George

*I now imbrace this oportunity
of writing you a few lines that you may no that i am well
i receaved your letter of the 28. I had begun to think
you had forgoten that i was on the Cape
and absent from my friends as i had writen*

and two weeks had past by and i receaved no answer

*i have about finished my visit on the cape
and wating for you to escort me home if convenant
if not please write imeadiatley
that i may not wait any longer
although i would not like to come a lone*

*it is late and i must close my letter
for i am fraid it will not go out in the mail
to morow. come iff you can George*

*Good By until we meet again
this from your friend Eleanor H Smith*

VICKI'S SOUP

i

velvety sheen of yellow
    swirled against the gloss of peppery red
  green cilantro runes
      dripped
     over

table desultory in circletalk, remember
    passepasse of planets
      a hand holding out a plate
remember this
   eight perfect mandalas

eating the art: slide of plangent color
              down burning

ii

a kitchen, the machinery of preparation
    afternoon in autumn colors
subtle and disarranged light

   sharpening to a focus
      a knife, a board, single sprig of green
overlooked
     as the doorbell rings

iii

is what is consumed
    in our living it
over,

or here now, still
              a lucent cup
         sacrament of human celebration
always,

    while
over liveoaks
    tallow trees
tipped drunken moon
         lights us home?

CHATEAU D'EAU

Only water tower, but how translated. Fluent
walls and mirrory turrets, misty outlines
of wet and polished stone, surfaces firm
but yielding, watery stairs to the tower.
Curtains of wind like gauze, grey faces
at the windows, wistful faces of the drowned,
of unborn children, of the waterwitch,
the lady of the lake, of Chateau d'Eau.

***

Yesterday in the glass wall of the gym
the pool's reflection overran the golf course,
wavelets in the grass. I watched it flow
where it wasn't, each green blade erect and dry
at the bottom of the shallow shimmering pond.
I was there too, my glasses glinted at me, my hand
moved with the pen, watching the surface tremble,
waiting for an ending, some great wave.

***

This afternoon the deluge caught me up,
a sudden cloudburst, just as quickly over.
      Now I stand in the true
           revision of weather, the air cooled off
smelling of earth and moss. I squint to track
    the runnels of dark water, study how
its own weight forms soft
         coils of it, unrolling,
     pulling away from itself, feeling out
      new grooves, extending itself

                    without pattern,
just looking for something
            until it's
                    gone.

I AM NO GARDENER

there beyond
the mossy sundial
how red the japonica
glistens in this
green rain
which slants across

the wood fence
gone grey
& even falling
away in places
but I leave it up
so I will not
disturb
the roses

which let alone
for years
took over
the west side
of the house
& must have come
to think of the place
as theirs.

DURING THE MUSEUM TOUR

You never know you're getting too much
of the Impressionists; they go down light
like millefeuilles, but lie
heavy in your gut like a tainted eclair.
Take this corridor of early Picasso—
You'll belch back the offtaste of blue
long after forgetting
his imaginary music.
Tomorrow in the supermarket
the bright red steaks will repel you,
the checkers will be sad clowns.
And in the afternoon
shadow will drench your porches.
Your pale children will call you
to walk with them in the sun.
Your ankles, wrists, and eyelids will be weights.

LA BELLE ANGÈLE (1889)

Marie-Angelique Satre, an innkeeper, was the subject of this painting. Thirty years later she said, "'Gauguin was very sweet and very miserable ... He kept telling my husband he wanted to paint my portrait, so one day he started ... but when he showed it to me, I said 'How horrible!' and told him to take it away ... Gauguin was crestfallen, and said that he had never painted such a good portrait ....'"

Deanna MacDonald,
http://www.worldsbestpaintings.net/artistsandpaintings/painting/137/

The face, closed,
eyes almost slits
keeping you away

that *beautiful* might be sarcastic
her body foreshortened and spread
rich embroidery of her dress

hat like a nurse, a nun, and
she an innkeeper's wife
busy with the chickens and the kitchen

that oval face, hair hidden beneath white
blue behind her, blue ornate Breton dress
for the feast, carven cold features

(it would have set her grandson up in business
had she politely accepted
put it away in the attic)

twisted gold statue to the left of her
was that she, was that distortion
her mirror image

her face her hands stained
with drabbled moist red light
she thought was kitchen blood

HERE

We spend our time building
or imagining fences. Still, things get in.

Tea at the righthand neighbor's, a widow
whose hair is growing out at last
from the tight crimps of married curls.
In the hard brown, intimations of soft silver.
Her hands less delicate too, nails torn
from garden, workshop, no more perfect halfmoons.

Tiny elaborate cakes on Spode.
But wine she made herself.
Ritual tea forgotten in the pot.

From the terrace room we watch the lazy dance
of sprinklers, the white deserted street.
The air glitters, empty lawn chairs lean
on trees like drunken aunts. What, wine,
wine in the morning?

Ralph always said, she says. But less affirmatively,
almost a question.
In our heads pass the remembered seasons,
the brief green spring, wheatcolored summer,
tans and yellows of fall, browns and blacks of winter.

Her sons are grown and gone. The table is set
for playing Patience, the longest game.

***

How the sun wears us out this summer,
its brightness more than its heat. The eyes hurt
for all the light. Eyes closed we dream the mountains
but would not live there, differently dwarfed.
The dogs, old enemies
lie down in the same shade.

Pampas grass consoles us,
greywhite plumes on stalks, bent in the wind.
These summer days they blow behind our eyelids,
asleep in daylight.

My mother visiting: "The sky here,
there's so much of it." And there is,
deep blue, rubbed to white at the edges.
Our brief afternoons a doll's tea set
spread out on a giant table.

**

we forget the places we came from, their different flowers,
the taller houses, people laughing at tables,
finetuned instruments and subtle colors.

And now at night
drifting above our beds
like steam above the tar backroads
we are a part of the place, are wholly here

(Or else 3 a. m. insomnia
draws us to the curtains.
Not a light on the street.
You miss the old neighbor
who used to work all night
in his shed, making God knew what
with power tools, faint sawbuzz

and drillwhine, muttering of the old
wornout sander
until sleep or dawn.)

***

On the widow's covered terrace
the vines have taken over, greening
the walls. I have not lived here quite long enough
to disappear into this largeness. She pours
more wine, shows me the new vases she's made
waiting for firing.
The pyracantha threatens the walks
her husband kept edged military trim.
The air is warming up, smells like moss, cut grass
and roses.

We talk. Spaces around us. Each.
Pampas grass. White puffs in wind.

GIRL MAKING A GARLAND (@1480)

This is a painting of desire,
of the twin desires to capture and be free.
She sits inside the open window,
long blonde hair flowing over the shoulders
of her orange gown. She looks down, calm, intent.
Above her a banner scrolls
"Ich pint mit vergis mein nit,"
I bind with
forget-me-nots.

Her wooden hoop drips flowers.
A white cat sits on the outside sill,
focused as she, but on
something in the foreground we don't see.
A single flower lies on the sill
but the cat cares nothing for it.
The cat is scraggly, no one's
pampered pet, he looks a little sad.

(Her lover waits for her in another painting.)
The frame of the window does not constrain
either girl or cat, each of whom
could any minute leap out,
run down the cobbled streets. But there
they stay, in yellow sixteenth century sunlight,

she weaving a crown of tiny flowers,
he watching the road.

FRA ANGELICO'S 'THE ANNUNCIATION' (@ 1448)

the mary and the angel are the same
sexless
   and only the angel's wings are real
you can touch them
                feel the wood and wax
arches repeat themselves like a dream of dreaming
while mary's hands and the angel's
     white and weightless
do not accept
   nor do they give the gift
which hovers in the air
           like unspoken words

the grass is deep the woods are wild as sin
from the small back room their rich dark light seeps in

THE ORCHARD

Photograph, 1902, Clarence White

One woman with her head
in the tree, hand reaching up,
another who fumbles a lower branch

and the third, bent down:
hoop extending the crushed skirt
hand in the dust,
settling for windfalls.

Women like collapsed gardenia blossoms—
three long dresses
two dark, one white,
rumpled, wilted, limp, unedited—

Does he pay them, the apple-pickers,
or do they do this for art,
the heavy, fusty dresses,
the sustained reach for the shutter's slow slide—

She gropes for something solid in the leaves
but there is nowhere
to put the apple she will pick.
This is clearly a pose
and only she, the central figure,
seems interested in apples
that can barely be distinguished in this picture,
sepia blobs, only a little
darker and fuller than the leaves.

Perhaps she will take them home
and slice them up with sugar for her children,
that afternoon's red gold.

ITALIAN NOCTURNE

Eugene Leslie Smyth 1857-1932

green smeared wall and the windows
barely distinguished and to the left the green
darkens to near black and in this Italian

village they are all asleep, every one
no candle or lamp in any of the windows
you can barely see but just the walls

and the dark shutters and the darker
uninterrupted sky, all the colors of black
but not completely peaceful, a bent dimness

a flicker as if in sleep
shadows catching at the lungs
a heat shriveling the webs of memory

no wind
no star
no light

THE HOME OF THE RADIOACTIVE CATS (1980)
(based on art by Sandy Skoglund)

in the home of the Radioactive Cats
an old trailer-dwelling couple
sets out supper, straight from the fridge
bread and cheese

the cats, glowing, green, rub against ankles
follow the old man
from the table to the rusty metal chair out front
on the makeshift porch
where he stokes his pipe

the cats, they're killing me anyway,
might as well smoke

the old woman scrapes off the plates
the cats play with the crusts
their bodies are almost transparent,
bulbous green muscles
arched green backs smooth green fur

(and here comes one now
delicate stealthy tread

(cautious ears
flattened against the head

(dreamcat, what are you stalking here
in the real?

NASTURTIUMS

"Rhoda Newman exhibited a watercolor... at the Pennsylvania
Academy of Fine Arts and gave her address as Commonwealth
Avenue, Boston. Nothing else is currently known about the artist."
(Notice below the painting)

Close to the frame's edge they are huge,
langorous, soporific,
despite their yellow, orange, reddish petals,
Toward the house they shrink to normal size.
Country cottage, long slope of red roof
far above the midpoint.

Below, apron of nasturtiums
spilling out of the frame
into my hands—

The loud bright clang of them,
their sexual curve and softness.
They undulate in an invisible wind.

The house inhabited (the curtains vaguely move)
but no one is in there now,
the woodshed is dark.

In the distance other chimneys
suggest community, but this house is apart,
owner gone, taking her name with her.

EDVARD MUNCH

It does not bear looking at long—
the furious dazzle, the orange boats

barely visible in violent roiling
waters, two black figures

heading down the deck, away
from the familiar icon

of anguish, without age, without
sex, waves of agony

distorting the hands, the head.
The sun was setting said Munch

and the clouds turned a bloody red.
I sensed a scream passing through nature.

Attempts to account for the picture:
he had agoraphobia,

he was drunk, he was insane, all
missing the mark, the plain sense of it:

A scream passed through nature.
Munch painted it.

FLOW

(Judy Chicago, Study for Birth Project, 1985))

No straight lines, not one.
only the breasts, buttocks, curled
parts of woman,
hills and valleys of woman,
no separations,
rippling curves, women gliding
over and into, out of
each other, themselves women
all motion and light
pinks, blues, reds, purples
coming out of their shadows
and behind them
something like a sun
rising over the nippled hill
her parts her whole
the all rolling
wet and breathless
into this cornerless world of women

LUM'S POND

what I thought then:
this is the opposite of Seurat's
un après-midi à la grande jatte here in Delaware

people spread out on dirty pebbles
looking at the pond
all facing the same direction

so long past and so many
of those gone who were there
your sister then barely grown

hot dogs burnt over coals
a nasty mixed-breed dog
mostly the sense of, *hey*

there was nothing else to do
and so we came here
but the water did look pretty

under the chilly sun and we took
a paddlewheel and patiently
propelled ourselves around in circles

sat down on the pebbles again
were bitten by this and that
proclaimed it a day and went home

forgot it until looking at Seurat
fifty years later brings it back, cancels out
the bites and rocks, rewrites

it all as happy

from ORDINARY SAINTS
St. Longjohn, the Pajama Saint

appealed to for protection by those
outdoors in their nightclothes,
shivering beside the burning hotel,

or going out at midnight
to shut the garage, and hearing
the door lock catch behind them,

or walking the dog
at 6 a.m.,
or just dashing out
because they caught sight of Venus
and Jupiter in the night sky

(it was much colder than she thought
but she stood there entranced
as the February chill blew through her

the two planets in their uncommon conjunction
and winter's touch on her cheeks, her thighs,
swirling under the hem of her wrinkled gown)

the saint (invent here his nocturnal life
and astounding martyrdom) raising his hand
in blessing to all those

who stand bathed in soft flannel, in moonlight.

St Langweil, the Saint of Those Waiting

(written while watching for the AAA on Route 290)

not, this time, for the biopsy result
or the news from the operating room

but just for anything: for the bus, for the next
available operator, for the line to crawl

slowly toward the desk of the DMV, for
the checkout (ice-cream melting,) for your friend

at the third-class restaurant, the waiter already
starting to look at you suspiciously, for

the traffic to snake past the freeway accident,
for the power to come back on

for a jolly muscular guy with a battery charger
and tow truck in case it doesn't work

just waiting in silence, you call forth the saint
of patience, of good humor, and you ask her

to be with you in the silence of your waiting,
not to let this hour be wholly wasted.

St Maytag, the Laundromat Saint

we strangers standing together
underwear whirling under glass
his jockeys jumping bodiless
her secret Victorias pinkly swirling

ask the patron saint of laundromats
to rinse away the loneliness,
guide sullen singles toward each other
across the grimy linoleum

let them raise their eyes to another's gaze
friendly and forgiving, taking in
dirty and clean, sorted and
unsorted, finding it all good

let them dream family and baby clothes
and their own proud machines
while these rented ones suds away evidence
of last night's boredom and excess

SAM'S

tired of no partner, wants
to snuzzle arse. Can't understand
a world of glass and sofas. Dreams
of feathers, fur, snapping bones,
taste of rancid meat. Doesn't like
the bland kibble, the canned boiled
beef. Gets stuck under the shed
chasing rats. Howls. Howls at the
moon. Howls at people embracing
genteelly on the chairs. Needs
dead skunks, filth to roll in. Chases
birds across the sky, bumps hard
into the fence, birds fly on free
beyond him. Lies stunned blank
on the mowed lawn, can't understand
any of it.

WATERPOEM

In this dream of thirst you drink the water
that never quenches though you gulp it
and pour it over you and it runs down your neck
pours off your arms but they are dry, dry
a sheen of liquid light sublimes to dust

On waking you find the flatness of water
that gushes from a chrome and plastic tap
tepid and tasteless like old routine
flowing between the hands and heart
toothbrush six o'clock suburban water

Where is the water that tastes new
like moss, like young potatoes
sliced into with an earth-encrusted knife
the water that moistens even into the veins
the gullies of the desert heart?

EXPLANATION

out there at night:
tiny pairs of eyes
in the azaleas,
behind the privet.

some think cats' eyes
really give light,
do not reflect
headlights, streetlamps.
few natural things
will shine like that,

but here there are
no cats.

those lucent points,
then, in darkness, those
are ghostcats. cats
gassed, shot
by stupid cowboys
from rotting porches.

these cats have names,
shadowwind, willothewisp,
stalkreed, featherbreath.
stand in your lighted
doorway and call them.

one by one
they shut their eyes
and disappear.

THE RED SWEATER IN THE SMITHSONIAN

So where is it kept, that we might visit it?
Has it its own closet, just a red sweater
swinging back and forth on a wire hanger

in the wind from a hidden vent, representing
the breath of Pittsburgh in the seventies, yours and
the Neighborhood's? Your soft serious voice

talking about dreams, pictures, magic,
about how we would never swirl down the hole
into the bowels of the city, where no one is special

and no one loves anyone. The later children
wanted paint guns and blasters, still they stopped
for awhile and listened. It was so quiet then

in the room with you, away from the kingdom of shout,
and we came back to see the same things happen
the same way over and over, the way the sweater

now swings in my head, edging a shoulder
now forward, now back, catching the wind;
now forward, now back, in the invisible wind.

HEINZ CHAPEL

Where I found the holiest place in the world,
better than Rome. Where Father Greene made me
a Catholic, told me about the Index of Forbidden Books.
Readers had to be pardoned by the Holy See,
not just their confessors. If I was going to read one,
he said I had to tear a page out first.

Where I was baptized with water from a shell.
Where fragments of colored light fell on my folded
hands, as I prayed to St. Anthony
to find my freshmen's exams, if he did
I would have no pizza for a month and put
the money in the Poor Box. He did. I did.

Where we lay out front, under cherry trees
And the petals drifted down on us. You: Did you sleep
With him? I: No. You: Why not? I: Because.
(I wanted so to be married in the chapel,
but parents, relatives chorused No! So I was married
in a home town church with stolid plain glass windows.)

Where I returned so many years later
and could not enter, shut out like Peter Pan.
They lock it! Now you can't get restless
at midnight in the dorm, walk a few hundred feet
across the delicious, blossom-scented dark,
slip through the door, fall to your knees, and pray.

FLOWERING CACTUS

on the front lawn
prickly pear grown wild in rainy weather—
like spiny driftwood, a gala float abandoned
from the elf parade, with papery yellow flowers

a sweet scent, paid for by sharp pain

why not mow over it? gallant pirate ship
with all flags flying, queening it on the
sea of green

dogs and cats stay clear
it flashes yellow, yellow in the passing motorist's eye
a child reaches out her hand, once only—

still the mower stops again at the edge
of the tiny fortress,
its flags and spires aligned in green rebellion

backs off,
veers left,
continues its broken path across the lawn

PHYSICS

There was something in the system
                despite its coldness,
something about the seventy-three bright chains
and the wavering points of light.
Across the infinite distances fell
      the patterns of fire
           shaped like triangles and hexagons.

Those of us who bought his kit
   could not fail to apply it,
though some had trees left over, and some had pistons,
      and no one could place the golden bird
to sing in its niche
   at the northernmost corner of being.

For anything so studied is serious.
   And this is the way the universe, in its
will to be understood
     fills these grooves
with silences like song.

NOON

Every man casts a shadow; not his body only, but his imperfectly mingled spirit. This is his grief. Let him turn which way he will, it falls opposite to the sun; short at noon, long at eve.
Did you never see it?

—Henry David Thoreau

ANSWERING MACHINE

I call my house, it's empty
and my own voice responds,
painfully hesitant, saying I'm
unavailable. I can hear
gaps in the apology, the whirring
tape, a stammer, a repetition,
an indrawn breath, then finally
and blessedly, the beep.

And I had redone that three times,
the first inaudible, the second
grammatically incorrect, and then
this one. I listen to the tape
recording silence, an expectant
hum, and I hang up.

If it was all that difficult
just to express absence,
then how can I begin
to tell you that I'm here?

LOST IN THE ZOO OF TO BE

The might-have-beens snarl,
Nip at each other's fur.
Zookeeper can't
Get them to mate. The is
And the are (who looks
Both ways at once) butt
Each other off the hill.
Has-beens are usually
Asleep, waken only
To meals, but the will-bes,
Muscular and sleek, pace
All day in their reinforced
Cages. The might-bes
Are the strangest, slimmest
Translucent animals,
You can not quite distinguish
Their stripes from the bars.
The grand old to-be
Himself, curled like a question,
Dozes in his imported
Tree, with one eye open,
Looking at what will happen
And what won't,
And at me, strange verb
Of uncertain tense, untethered.

PASCAL AT THE RACES

1

The Gambler: there he is in the old cartoon,
florid and
shiny-eyed,
clutched handful of cards.
Other hand in his pocket, groping for
what: an ace, some money,
a gun, a handkerchief
to mop the sweat?

I don't know you, Sir, but you are scary,
with your handful of aces, your possible gun.

The college argumentation competition:
mode: Inspirational.
Back row spectator, my mild speech on reading
not having got itself written, and here comes a Valkyrie
on Gambling. Wild shaggy hair, she pounds the stage.
points and accuses.
Children dying of want, wives gone to the streets.
Visual aids: empty-eyed man in prison
uniform, corpse found in the lake.
Graph falling, red line down and out.
Bingo's almost as bad, it leads to this.

I am in the back. All Catholics gamble.
She gets first prize.
The speech I would have bet on
describes Creative Loafing and doesn't place.

2

wind and horse-stink
here they come:
Charley's Mane, Poker Chip,
Razzmatazz.

I bet on the favorite
always, to show:
pick up $2.20
on my $2 bet.

winning's what counts,
not how much,
no such thing
as a little winner.

3

my granddaughter takes her first step,
the floor rises to strike her, she's astounded,
the cry collects itself in her throat.

she was betting on air,
thought it was thicker, believed in it,
it would hold her up, protect her
from the violence of the floor.

4

Consider a golden horse on an infinite track,
hooves hitting the line at regular intervals.
You could plot its course,
predict its arrival at point A, point B
to the second. This would be expressible graphically
and no one would bet against you.

Would you bet that 2 + 2
would equal seventy-three?

Here in the text is a picture of the mathematics of chaos,
its coils, brilliant in colors,
the dimensions of chaos,
a chart of the contents of chaos,
a list of the contents of chaos.

5

"Infinite—nothing. Our soul is cast into a body, where it finds
number, time, dimension. Thereupon it reasons, and calls this
nature, necessity, and can believe nothing else."

6

smell of beer & peanuts,
sweat & hard luck.

bet every cent on the longshot
& there he is in the last race
just pulling ahead, out of the crowd,

now a length beyond the others, faster & lighter.
looks like he could fly,
take right off from the track,

headed there now, here now, home.

THE NURSERYMAN

In the last spring of your life
You sat in a wicker chair
Exhausted, sunshade down,
While all your gardens ran amok:

The columbine invaded,
Its reds and purples rioted
Down your stern rows of arbor vitae,
Crabgrass and jasmine
Overgrew the grey slates
Of your garden path, all
Direction was lost,
The unclipped privet
Reached out across the rutted road,
Wisteria grappled your horse-chestnut trees,
Wildly growing dewberries
Blocked your kitchen door.

You were not awake to see
Forsythia take over your potting shed,
Spilling into it like sunlight.

READING THE CIRCULAR

the gravestones are like cars in a used car lot
different styles, colors, shapes
to cruise across a sea of green

I need to choose ours today
(yours now, I will be along)
perhaps this brown red one, long as a boat

or the bright red one, festooned with flowers
could be a Mardi Gras float, or maybe
the brick one, solid as a tow truck

strangely they all have the wife's last date
open, as if no men are choosing these
and none of them have angels or winged skulls

but most have marble roses, linked rings
how strange we are, I'll special-order angels
one for each of us, surely among the artists

there must be some old guy who can carve angels

KLIMT'S GARDEN

An indifferent garden, dwarfed by the severe house
With its curtains drawn. He could be a monk
Standing before it in his oversized smock,
Statue-like on the rough pebbled path,
Gazing at glossy leaves and a few flowers.
But in his painting every flower breathes.
The garden pulses, overflows with verve,
Firewheels nudge the margins, white asters
Burst with life like stars. This is an infinite garden,
Where the canvas ends, the growth goes on,
Tendrils, rhizomes groping beneath the wall,
Greening the space, hinting at lines and links
Between us all and forever, while the real Klimt
Stands on the next page contemplating his garden,
Dark, regular. Arms folded over his smock, seeing
What he sees.

FORBIDDEN IMAGES

over her shoulder Lot's wife looking back
at the home she was leaving, wanting to glimpse
for one last time the field, the goats, dogs, hens,
her old father waving at the gate.

but she turned into grief itself, a statue of grief,
a columned tear. and then
Eurydice, who herself did no wrong
but Orpheus could not wait for her to form
herself in the world, and looked, and so lost her,
her slender weeping ghost melting away
into the underworld. and still more:

Diana in her bath,
the bronzed young hunter
seeing her, stunned, fascinated,
then turned into a stag, hunted down
by his own dogs. and then you, curious one,
wanting to see, to name. if you knew

a face wreathed with snakes would calcify you,
but you knew it would hold perfect, consuming beauty,
each of your cells bursting as they turned
into the purest light: would you
not look?

HOTEL

I take off my clothes and hang them up,
I bathe in the soapy water and towel off
with the thick white towel, I watch myself
in the full-length mirror, my old white body
with all the dents and wrinkles. I walk nude
in the deep carpet, feeling light and young.
I take off my skin and hang it in the closet.
my form is a dim outline now, I can throw
my curtains wide to the city, no one can see me.
In a thousand windows people are dancing,
eating, opening bags, and making love.
I am dissolving now, part of the air,
the night sky, this city unknown to me.
My vague form drifts over the bed,
sinks into the duvet. Tomorrow another woman
will don the skin and clothes, walk out the door,
someone I've never met.

AFTERNOON

"There is an hour of the afternoon when the plain is on the verge of saying something. It never says, or perhaps it says it infinitely, or perhaps we do not understand it, or we understand it and it is untranslatable as music."

—Jorge Luis Borges

FRONTIER

Toilets and committees vs
        rattlesnakes.
The feel of surfaces, birthing a calf, your hand in her belly, or cutting wood. Raw sound of the saw, splinters and shavings, smell of green wood, of sap, cut branches.
No path, until you walk there.
Words shrunk to necessity, commands, announcements.
    OK, pine, glue, died, now.

It was a heavy line, a pipe
pushed forward by men and animals
until the ocean stopped it.
Theft of course but driven, a blind mole.

Sunk in the water there, the great forest
      falling behind it into lumber.
Yet something is padding the outline of the sea,
        desperate, forgotten.

My life already curling, sepia, inward.

TRANSLATION EXERCISE

There is the woodcutter's hut
next to the figures by Hummel.
The small boy looks sweetly astonished.
He does not see the end of the fairy tale.

*Es scheint als ob das Frühling
dieses Jahr nie kommen wird.*
Patches of snow melting
into the dark earth,
the mist on the mountain.

It seems as though this year
spring will never come.

The boy, patiently chopping wood,
and the seasons rolling by

In der Natur fängt das Jahr am ende Marz an.

Here in town, though, in der Stadt
we hardly notice the seasons.
They used to fast during Lent.
Summer replaces spring before we know it.

*Die Sonne geht je früher auf, und ehe wir daran
denken, ist der Sommer hier.*

*Die Sonne kehrt in ihrer Bahn um, und die Tage werden immer
kurzer.*

Is it that the earth rolls faster
or that time just seems shorter
as you get older.

Während des Herbstes verliert die Erde
viel von der Sommerwärme.

You learn better by repetition.
As you age, something hardens,
it takes more and more pressure to cut the grooves.
The earth loses its warmth
from the outside in.
At last even the center will be cold.

The boy's breath makes a cloud,
his arms are tired from woodcutting.
There should be quite a pile of wood
after all these years, we should have learned something
of the language of the earth.

REDEMPTION

I don't remember dreams, but I did this one.
I arrive at my old house with the slanted drive
and I leave my truck without setting the brake
thinking I'll just be a minute, but
as I step off the drive it starts up,
zips backward down the driveway
and crashes into the car across the street.

A metal bang like a great bomb going off
and I see the two cars tangled together
in a clump of twisted metal. I want to run
but set my shoulders, walk across the street,
the wreck growing bigger, more complex
as I pass it. Now it looks like two
airplanes jammed together, maybe three.

I knock tentatively, then louder,
wondering why no one has come to the door,
because I hear faint music and soft voices.
But then a woman comes through the side gate
in a silk dress. I point to the wreck,
hand her my insurance, but she laughs,
looks at the huge ruin, says not to worry.

She says there's a party out back and I
absolutely must come. *Don't be concerned
about the cars, we'll sort that, just come in.*
Confused, I follow her through the gate
into a yard much bigger than I'd thought.
It's an English garden—odd for central Texas—
full of everyone I've ever known, wearing

everything from workout clothes to bikinis
and they seem glad to have me join them.
Distant piano music drifts toward me
and the drinks are silvery, vague and satisfying.
I worry about the wreck but its image fades
as we walk along the paths among the flowers.
I don't remember dreams, so why, then, this one?

SHOP WINDOW: THE FASHION IN BRUSSELS

behind the gleam of glass, the dark assembly

the twelve figures
   browns and blacks
      woolen coats and snoods

scarves and stockings
   brimless hats of felt
      gloves of tarnished silver

a hand held back
   a casually held purse
      a hand reaching

bodies in full cover for the season
   backlit   smooth featureless faces
      turned from the noisy street

graceful wooden limbs
   in an uneven row
      dressed appropriately

for some cold occasion
   heads modestly aligned
      in disciplined acceptance

of the formal coming of winter

ii

at my sunny doorstep
soundless footsteps,
a choreographed arrival.

briefcases, polished black
leather. I open the door,
they stand expressionless,

faces remote. bald sun burning
cracked earth, dry tangle of vines.
flakes of light fall on their heads.

what have you come
halfway round the world
to sell me?

*this is the postwar style
of Europe, few can afford it.*

a mere glance tells them that
I cannot, they turn as one
to leave,

and though I call out wait,
I have credit, they have already reached
the street, one throws

a negligent silver scarf
over an elegant black shoulder.

iii

a dozen dark-clad figures playing,
throwing snowballs! In Texas August!
how gracefully they heft the missiles back
to throw, the tall one leaning forward,
the twins playing catch. a shorter figure
(at far left) cupping her hands,
forming a ball. could that be laughter,
the sound in the wind like aspen leaves,
like fluttering paper?

I DON'T

I don't remember my dreams these days, just
an impression, maybe a scene,
usually of departure.

usually of departure, I am
supposed to be packed, but too much remains
lying around, clothes, pictures, books.

lying around, clothes, pictures, books,
and I want to take all of it with me
but I am late for the train,

but I am late for the train
and there is an endless warren of gray tunnels
through which I run, my life falling around me

and I have to run, my life falling around me
from the two battered old suitcases
that were stuffed to bursting

that were stuffed to bursting
and the gray train starts to move and I jump
aboard, spilling underwear and spices,

aboard, spilling underwear and spices,
as the train picks up speed and I look around
thinking, surely there's nothing left,

thinking, surely there's nothing left,
when the train rockets out into unknown landscape
and I drop the empty bags to lift my eyes.

PEELING

Epidermis flakes from my fingertips,
knuckles, even the heel of my hand.
Dermis too in places. My touch sandpapered,
everything an irritant. Touching others

painful now, too little skin
between us. My reddened hands
scalped, scalded, excoriated. I feel
her arm, it is a wall. My rawness hurts,

my hard shell gone. If you were still here
I could touch you, my pain against yours,
a kind of knowledge. There are people
like that, transparent, others crowd them,

to know them conveys reality
but the others use them up, the transparent beings,
wanting to hold them, breathe them, make them theirs,
until there is nothing left of them but light.

NINETEEN THIRTY-SIX

(For Pauline Hanschitz Lacey, 1916-1986)

Masses of greys and blacks. Trees? Clouds?
Indistinct shadings. A house? A hill?
*O Mum, look how incredibly beautiful
it is, the Neckar dividing
the hills, see that tree
reaching from the hillside like an arm?
We picnicked there this noon. I'm nibbling
on leftover grapes now, so those spots
are grape juice, they're not tears!* The letter
dated June 18, l936, sixty years ago
exactly to this day. I take my bifocals off,
squint at the tiny photograph. The arm?
The tree? Die Universität Heidelberg?
I'll never forget this year, ever.
These shadows must be hills.
This dark patch, your gloomy roommate
you called Schopi, for Schopenhauer.
So says the letter, no one now could tell.

But in my head you're in color. How sorry I am
we never made home movies. No, I'm glad.

Thirty years ago on our schemed-for,
long delayed vacation
stout by then, you chatted with the maid
in the Nice hotel, learned the manager
used the leftover rolls and checked the maid's
old purse each day "Though I've never taken anything!"
She stuck the job because her *p'tit ami*

took care of the cars. The pebbled beach
was blinding white. Can you be half a tourist,
half a guest? Can someone's wife
be anything but tourist? The maid came from
a tiny hamlet, had never been to Paris. To her
you were Madame.
At twelve I studied languages
    je rêve, tu rêves, il rêve
  It is different for a child, dreaming in French
touching the maps, the different colored spaces,
Jacques et Louise picking flowers, *innocents au jardin*
    ich träume, wir träumen, er träumt
A German dream is resonant like a drum.

Your rusty whisper amid hospital noises,
beeping monitors, hiss of oxygen,
carts whirring by, televisions
in all the rooms: *Marge, we were
so stupid.* I held the phone to your ear,
repeated your words to your high-school best friend.
She was crying, an old lady now in New Jersey, you said
she was still beautiful.   So stupid.   Not to
get together? Only to write at Christmas?
You spoke so carefully, still I could hardly hear.
I held your hand, the left one with the ridges
where the rings had been so long. We never found them.
Dad said how little it matters, how little
anything matters, I remember
the day we chose them.

The little priest held our hands,
he prayed, but not that you would
live, would that be impious then? Or only foolish.
We said Amen, a circle round your bed. Your hands
white as the holy bread.

And these are the colors of the Seven Sacraments:
Baptism is white
Confirmation is pink
Matrimony is red
Holy Orders are brown (varying shades of brown)
Penance is grey
Extreme Unction is black
Holy Eucharist is blue
No sacraments are green, that is the faerie color
It is hard to distinguish extremes of blue from black
I cannot draw a line
between the black and the very darkest blue

A photograph of faces—this one perfect, though there's a fine
network of cracks in the glaze, as in old porcelain.
First under the light: George Holland
2nd row: Schopi, The Weird One, Jim, Karl,
The fellow with the turban and the moustache
is the Egyptologist. You are not there.

But I would sing you back, Orpheus
of the stumbling tongue, here at the cave's dark lip
so I slide the drawer open
you locked yourself in all these years, and see a face
younger than my daughter's, a slim dark-eyed girl
a translucence on the skin, everything to happen:

We arrived at Hamburg at five o'clock. A grey
day, everything had that hazy Autumn look
I love so much. The lights circled with mist
and the glare of the shops subdued to a glow. Ben
and I wandered the streets, he nearly
destroyed the romance by commenting on exactly
how much everything would cost in the States. Mum,
how easily I could feel at home here!

You were so definite. Make love not war. Draft beer
not boys. Defending your language students
from principals and police. Signing up
everybody to vote, letting them register
all their relatives, teaching French
to the neighborhood ladies in your living room,
iced tea circles ignored on the Queen Anne table.
But this girl is uncertain, does not yet walk
your decisive tread, does not even wear glasses.
There are the letters, the photos faded
past all help, the clippings from the Heidelberg
paper I can't read, the whole year
you never told me about. (I did not ask.
I was stupid, anyway
you did not want to tell me.) A tiny leather folder
like a scapular, with your parents' photos, and behind
your father's, another, of a blonde-haired German boy
in an army uniform.

> in the dreams you clutch the gift against dawn
> desiring to bear it safely into day,
> but it dwindles in your hands
> your fingers blindly clutch the empty light
>
> if you only could. as in the children's stories
> a token, something always left in the palm
> solid talisman to prove the irrational, QED magic

I hold these faded leaves, vivid arrows in my blood

*Mum, bei Beyer ist's so gemütlich! Schopi
and I roasting apples and nuts in our hundred-fifty
year-old porcelain stove, how many roasted
apples it must have seen! Can you believe the Beyers
greet each other mornings with Heil Hitler.*

*twenty years married and no one looking. How these people
love parades! We saw one yesterday
through the streets of Heidelberg. Nazis are pretty
to look at. Don't believe what you hear, though,
no one here wants war. What nonsense people
do talk! I've met a student
in the regular German army, his name's Hans,
he's helping me a lot. What a complicated
language, seems to be all growls and snorts.
How I miss you! Get Marge to wear the dresses
and mark the box Gebraucht, that way there'll be
no duty.*

in the hospital you said, *take my purse,
I want you to have it.* But there were thirty-four,
one in every drawer, every closet

Those wrecked handbags like cars
rusting out in junkyards,
cruising all the eras of your life

& I saw the maitre d's
rushing from the doors
of all the inns of Europe

*Gnädige Frau, haben Sie etwas vergessen
Madame, votre sac à main*

happy in your pleased confusion
they basked in your apology
bowed and waved as you left
those purses, they came back every time
like pets who knew the way

Take my purse

So many ticket stubs
notes addresses schedules
gloves combs programs
an overflow of generous
extravagance

I want you to have it

Old ones with silver dimes
& lace handkerchiefs

New ones with electronic
bank cards & calculators

all our shopping binges
blouses bought for me, handed over
in a flurry of lace & laughter

This oldest one, a flimsy leather pouch
limp as a wet chamois, holding only
a bus token, a Reichsmark

The day after you died the Challenger went up.
Mute and frozen we watched it on TV all day,
exploding time after time, again and again the looks
of triumph changing to horror, the bright
flare in the sky, the plume of smoke, the fall.
No one said anything. The phone rang and rang.
People brought food, they came and left, the long hand
crawled around the clock.

    I look at Hans' picture, am I doing wrong?
    A violator of graves, playing with dust,

Trying to read the void?
How vanished is a fifty-year-old kiss, it leaves
no spot on the page. He looks kind and earnest.
He had a schloss in Ziegelsdorf, your letter
said, I study his homely face,
imagine the grey plane of his cheek flushed
with mountain air, you tracing with your finger
the angles of his face. Did you tell him
you loved the October's apple scent and clear
cold light, did you tell him
you would come back, did you ever say
Ich liebe dich?

If I could close my eyes and wish, tear through the grey
tissue of time, taste his lips, hear his words,
your words. Time is a fence across the endless field,
an arrow on the blank, a sequence of pearls.
Your finished life, a clasp at either end.
    That vacation, we broke bread with your Austrian
    relatives and then said Du.
    Die alte Beti, Kaufmann Heinz, around the table
    they told their lives. You did not
    want to go back to Heidelberg, Dad took you,
    you barely raised your eyes up from the guidebook.

Why I said.
It's so different, you said, *it's not what I remembered*.
We went into the Konditorei and had strawberry tart with whipped
    cream. It was Sunday, the Catholics were all coming
    from the Peterskirche. I said *where did you stay*.
You said *I don't remember*, your eyes veiled.

Mum, today I bought a bicycle, it was 18
reichsmarke or $4.65! Everyone rides
to Mannheim to the opera, you can get a seat

*for 15 cents in the back row. It's about
3/4 hr. ride. The bicycle, I call her
The Iron Duchess. This afternoon we rode
up in the hills to the ruined tower— Schop was inclined
to climb up and look at it, but it seemed
so romantic from the road, it would have been a shame
to examine it more closely. This is the most
beautiful place—and thank you so much for the
package! I just carollted, gebraucht, gebraucht,
and tanzte past the astounded Offizielle—*

So few are ready, your old Mum perhaps,
past ninety and the lights turned out,
deliveries discontinued, all the letters addressed
and stamped. And yet. . .

*Another parade! The man up at the head
so far away, I could not see him, I am not sure
who he was or what all this means. But what
enthusiasm! And Mum, dear, the cake
I had this noon—a whole mark it cost, my greatest
extravagance so far, I could have had lunch and dinner
at the Mensa Academica.*
  *The top layer was chocolate
  then a layer of almond cream
  then raspberry jam
  then a layer of chocolate again
  then something crunchy like toffee
  hazelnut cream
  more chocolate*
*I do believe it is the most delicious thing I have ever eaten.
But don't worry, dear, about my pocketbook or waistline, I'll never
do it again. You might send in the next package
some Butterfingers— look for them at Williams'
chocolate-covered crunch in yellow packages, a penny
each I think.*

Mother I am reading your letters
by the light of your old lamp, a yellow light
on yellowed pages. I think you would like that.
But how long do you live after you die?
Three years or five? How long do they remember
that you loved balloons, how long do they call forth
from their fluttering, dying cells
the timbre of your voice?

    The vacation guidebook said
    if a German gave you anything
    you were to respond by saying, "Donkey Shane."
    You loved that. "Shane," you said,
    for the cup, the toast, the shawl,
    the glimpse of the Schwarzwald. Shane,
    we said it always afterward, Shane
    for everything.

Mum, your Babs can do more stupid
things in a week that you could dream! Hans
and Peter and Wilfried and I went out to Peter's
mother's place and looked at baby dachshunds. Afterwards
Peter said joking, won't you take one home
and I said I'd take two, name one Heil
and the other Hitler. Everyone's face froze
but Hans', he just looked confused, and I
realizing what a brick I'd dropped, chattered
about American cigarettes until Wilfried said
I must go now, in a stiff voice, and left,
and Peter left too. Later Peter left a message
with Frau Beyer to uninvite me to dinner that night.
Hans said he didn't want to go there
anyway, what a bore. I guess I'll learn to be
more careful. Things are so serious here—
even all those parades, corps after corps,

the SA, the RA, the regular army, the Hitler Mädchens,
the Hitler Jugend, marching grimly on
one after another— I hope I'll learn.

In the dream the Nazis are chasing me over the hills,
shouting to each other in a ferocious language
and shooting. Dodging bullets and shrapnel, I run
for the border, a tattered map in my hand.
I know if I come to the line dividing
Germany from France, I'm safe, home free.
But then I find the line—and it's the edge
of blackness, on the other side nothing,
no light.   Despairing, I look up to see the Nazis
nearly upon me, screaming victory, and suddenly
I know it's all okay! It's only that I have
the wrong map! I look over the terrain
and the light and the dark part are all marked off
in zones of light and dark, dots, circles, broken lines,
the land mapping itself. Now the Nazis are frozen
like war-statues of bronze, their shrieks
etched in the metal. Over there on the dark side
some animals are awakening, friendly polar bears
with silvery fur.

Mum, Schop's aunt sent her
Of Time and the River—I've been all day reading—
he writes so like the way I feel at times,
the description of October, my favorite month,
almost unbearably true.   I guess I'd never make
a German Frau. Hans and I hiked to the Ehrenfriedhof,
you can see miles and miles, even the Rhine
and the French frontier. Lunch at the Königsstuhl
Gäststatte, so many lovely flowers! I wish I knew
their names.

Hans and Paulina then, amidst the early spring
flowers, they kiss
tentatively, she stops thinking
of the German word for kiss. Bees are dive-bombing
the black-eyed susans, the air is thin and bright.
She is wholly there, caught, caught up
in the embrace, nothing left over
for Mum and Dad back home. She learns
his rough cheek, his tobacco smell, his taste,
his hands bring her flesh to life, the air
alive around her.
Surely somewhere this is happening,
below the tissue of time, surely you've seen them
in the WWII movies, the cleareyed couple in the mountain cafe,
his rumpled collar, her dark strong face, a glass of wine.

O Mum, the German Märchen-haunted
woods, the loveliest in the world!
I shall never forget them.
It will be so hard to leave, I long
for you and dad, though, and your dear
disorderly garden. Despite my lack of cash
I'm bringing you a fine print of Van Gogh's
Sonnenblumen—it's haunted me all year
in the art shop window. The colors are perfect
for over the piano—if you have the right
yellow candles, the room will be quite lovely.
If only I could stay a month or two. Hans is here,
eating cherries—wanting me to finish up
my scribblings and go with him— Dear, I must dash.

Evenings your hospital room filled up
with liquid orange light. The nurse I hated,
who shouted as though you were deaf, came on.
We ignored her, talked the long night through
mostly with handclasps. Eight squeezes meant I love you.

I never tried in German. Old movies
and reruns flickered on TV. Once more they opened up
the safe on the Andrea Doria. You dozed, I watched,
tiny voices barely audible.

  and history goes down like that,
      in orange light. the glittering house
         lit up one last time
  with a million candles,
     the dream of revelry inside,
        some age
         blown out
  the last gleam dulled and gone

The opening: lire and dollars matted
together, sodden lumps. Nothing.
TV cameramen, everyone
pretending there must still
be something: is that a glint of diamond?
no, only the spotlight on
black water. Credits flash across the screen.

Earlier: the man and woman of the
expedition, come back. Tanned, not young,
lined faces of old merman, mermaid.
He said, this was a dream, all those years
I've waited. She said, don't open it.

Eurydice at the mouth of the cave,
warmed almost to life. Lukewarm pale being.
Don't look. She's only there
if she isn't.

Earlier: the eels circle the
crusted pipes, masses of kelp drift

through the ruined twisted rooms.
Divers intrude, step precariously
over the rubble. Ceilings are walls,
walls are floors.

Hands picking up cups, plates
wiping away green sludge, exposing
ordinary trademarks.

then/now: the lid rises slowly,
a mermaid is in the box, crowned with gold.
She shakes her head sleepily and smiles.

then/now: the stone within
suffuses the chest with a dim glow. All the cameramen
stand back agape

   And here: your shallow breath,
   the wavelets on this shore receding

Old newsreels in my head, fifties faces,
the strangeness of circumstance,
of accident. The child saved
who should have died, flung
from one ship to another. The child lost
who should have lived, dropped
into the hands of strangers.

pain, loss
faces yellowing, curled
at the edges like these pages,
gone, swept away

     and what of that other
     goodbye? a kiss, a promise?
          no letters.

two years later, a wedding
    my father
        me

      I opened the hospital
blinds. slats of sky and stars
    fell across your bed, the winged
        lights hovered over the parking lot
a car coughed, starting up in snow

the fish swimming in the skewed rooms
glide behind the crisscross tubing
in their violated home

  You sang, *Du, du, liegst mir im Herzen,*
  du, du, liegst mir im Sinn
  Last morning in the hospital: dawn light
  coming thinly in through the walls,
  diffusing through the bricks outside,
  the sheetrock, the plaster, into the room

to dive for what then? gold?
something must come back, must
be brought back, Eurydice, rising

  in the red smog of Stalingrad
  no one remembers one of the last to fall,
  an American girl's picture in his pocket, or

the wealthiest dentist in Hamburg, fat wife
and two fat daughters. sometimes between patients
thinks about the years before the war. will not retire

Of his bones are coral made

"My greatest fear," says the old merman,
is that bacteria may have destroyed
the contents of the safe, while it was guarded
by sharks in the fish tank. Cold water
preserves, warm destroys. Do you recall
the letters in the Lusitania, quite legible
after all those years?"

"Sir, 1956 was a good
year, will you drink the wine?"

They think the rubies
in this ruined frame are genuine
but to find out for sure, they would need
to destroy the frame. Thus we will leave them.
They may be rubies.

   Old Hans, smiling, welcomes me to his Schloss
   which turns out to be the castle
   from the frontispiece of your old books,
   My Book House, where I first learned to read.
   The nobles and the peasants, parents, children,
   trailing up the hundreds of stone steps
   to the tower— is it a cloud castle
   or is it real, somewhere along the Rhine?
   His eyes, his voice, his face are so
   familiar, surely I have been here once,
   our lives are woven with such skill
   into the tapestries that line the walls.

Merman and mermaid,
      holding hands and singing,
they sing you almost real
  before the spell is lost.
Eurydice waits in the cave,
pale and gold.

    Mother, there are further
and deeper rooms in your house. Blurred forms
    move even now on this watery threshold,
their shadow outlines sharpening.

MY FATHER'S HOUSE

(For Edmund M. Lacey, 1913-1988)

my parents' house waits to be sold
with my father's shoes still in it,
in the closet, size thirteens

and here the shoes beside my bed
fill up with darkness every night,
when I get up I chase away the darkness
with my thrusting feet

shoes are so much more intimate
than underwear
holding the sweat and ridges,
shape of anklebone and arch

'86, after Mother died,
rack after rack of shoes
twinned, waiting, expectant
put into the goodwill bags

(and who will walk in my silence,
wearing my silence)

vacant house 2000 miles from here.
clocks ticking on the walls,
the electronic surveillance system
with the button you did not push
red and green lights blinking like Christmas

and I here, and the dreams
oh, the dreams. If I could say,
come back, I will not run away this time,

I will not run away to the flat brick house
and the children shrilling around the table

shoes, silence, stairs, empty rooms

daguerreotypes, tintypes:
a blond child in a long Cossack coat
with a horse on wheels beside him,
his fair face a flaccid sweetness,
greatgreatgrandfather noname with his grandson's face,
my father's face, my son's who bears his name

******

I have looked in every crevice of the past,
and nothing was there,
though the old photographs were webbed with light,

though the light splintered in my hands
though I bear the gashes now, invisible wounds
bleeding light,

nothing, no one was there

******

only a month ago you said, "This was a good house,
you never liked it.
But I'm glad I never left it."

only last year you finally told me you were the one

who found your father:
"he was still alive, the hole in the middle
of his head.
he was gasping, you know, like this."

I walked ahead of you into my house.

******

after Mother died I used to dream
I came home and you both welcomed me,
it was only later I noticed something was wrong,
some wrong thing, unidentifiable...
you could not remember which of you was dead,
but agreed that you wanted me to stay, I could not leave.

outside your house the air is full of petals,
fronds from the trees are drifting over the steps.
drifting over the porch, fronds and dogwood petals,
past the For Sale sign, like snow.

someone will live there, a couple
with a baby perhaps. Some child will walk down the path
as I did, hopping from flagstone to flagstone,
into the darkness of the line of trees.

for him the trees will fill
with dancing points of light,
the honeysuckle, the forsythia will draw him,
he will see faces in the branches, maybe yours.

******

If you could say "I'm sorry" to the dead,
just that: "I'm sorry"
and just once

If the dead could be satisfied, and not stand
in the dark like that, waiting and judging and reaching
If they could be satisfied, if we could sing them to sleep

sorry about the boy in 1926 who went out to the barn
sorry about the sea of whiskey
sorry about my pontius pilate hands

which know touching the keys now how futile this is
this empty music

I will leave my gift there at the line of trees,
a song I know is only for myself,
to sing myself to sleep

✶✶✶✶✶✶

in our parents' house the grass grows kneedeep,
we are safe in this room there are no snakes
we play hideandseek
hiding in the ormolu clock
it is always eleven o'clock here the sun
not yet in the middle of the sky

creek water drips down a curving staircase
we are old now the Edwardian sofa
grows into the floor and the names
of the games we play we cannot even remember
red rover turns to statues in the sun

the moss grows on the north side of the piano
where the keys stick on the same tune, Broken Journey
the glass grapes take over the western wall
while we bury gilt rings in the Persian rugs
mud oozing between our fingers

✶✶✶✶✶✶

in the dream they are there at home, in the house,
and I am coming back late, from something, the movies,
the prom. Mother is sitting up
with a cup of cocoa, asking, did you have a good time?
Dad is out walking the dog. At 1 a. m.? But this is a dream,
we are all relaxed and happy, no one is drunk,
no one is weeping and nothing is wrong or strange.
my boyfriend's white Mercury convertible
circles the block once, honks goodbye

bebebebeep, goodbye

going upstairs I pass the case
where my father's grandfather's lead soldiers
are ranged in rows. I pick one up.
this is the Boer war, where my other great
grandfather died

The soldier is carrying
a battered standard, suddenly I see
the wound in the head, the blackened blood

I let him drop

he lies in the corner of the stairwell,
against the polished grain of the wood
his wound is bleeding into the wood
gushes of dark blood

******

"Four hundred dollars," the antique dealer says,
but I cannot. They lie in the cigar box
gathering dust, their tiny banners bent.

But I wrote "gathering dusk." A keystroke undid it.

They lie there gathering dusk
like my shoes beside the bed,
duskgathering. I cannot sell

If you could be satisfied

but I never could sing, tonguetied and fevered
in the fifthgrade pageant, you were there in the
third row.
I was Katrina of Hanover City. You were there.

I found the stories I hated, the little match girl
the lead soldier and the fir tree
all the sorrows in the attic under the eaves,
boxes of soldiers and even the wheeled horse
of your grandfather's picture,
but where were the stone blocks?

they were cool, deep shades of red and blue,
lattices and windows, arches and chimneys,
the city we built was real.
boats sailed under the stone bridges,
towers kept the orphaned princesses.

the finished city touched with sunset
immanent, a radiance
come in now, put away the blocks
come in now, put away the blocks

Come in now, put away the blocks.

******

What is more blackandwhite
than a death certificate? *Blunt head trauma.*
Now the word "blunt" becomes a kick in the stomach,

not a big laughing fellow telling me
I'm unbuttoned. *Accident,* they said. The police kindly
and puzzled, over the wire. The empty pints,
the blood. *Investigation. Autopsy.* Not words
in my language, but I learn them.

And take the soldiers home, some of them broken,
shields missing, or arms, they lie in the cigar box
all the wars tangled together, defeated. Things,
what good are things? What do they know? The house
is a vacuum, a void,
sucking me in from 2000 miles away.

My better angel says, sell the soldiers,
give away the shoes and walk out barefoot.
You cannot say you're sorry or goodbye.
Feel the grass soft on your naked soles
that the dark may rest more lightly on your shoulder.

The soldier heavy, silent in my palm.

THE SPIDERS OF CHERNOBYL

spin crazy webs, wild, raggedy loops
with threads hanging, holes, overlaps.
they spin in the dark hinterland of disaster.

scientists chase after them with cameras.
they may be mutants, spinning
the disordered webs, no two alike,
but not like snowflakes, asymmetrical.

knitters gone mad, casting, recasting.

spiders in her head
spinning irregular paths
shiny disconnected strands
hanging on tattered debris of thought.

sunshine through the stunted trees of chernobyl
turn the words to silver.
broken letters of shattered alphabets
knit knots.

scientists in space suits
poking her synapses.
cameras click.

maybe a smooth beginning
and then strands farther and farther afield
ending in a tangle, a dot.

these are the radioactive fields
of the burnt globe, and the spiders,
the spiders of Chernobyl are spinning their webs.

EVENING

Let us go then, you and I,
When the evening is spread out against the sky . . .

—T. S. Eliot

Friendship is the shadow of the evening,
which increases with the setting sun of life.

—Jean de La Fontaine

The evening star is the most beautiful of all stars

—Sappho

REPORT TO THE ASSESSOR-COLLECTOR

Dear Sirs: I am at a loss
to explain
the absolute disappearance
of so large
an item.

Use in a sentence: disappearance, disappointment, adolescence.

An appointment
without a point, a dis
appointment.
The pistol lies on the cracked walk,
spent caps smell like salt.
(This belongs in an earlier poem. Delete.)

She wrote "We do not want
to loose you,"
and so we remained there,
shackled to her shadow.

We are no doubt still there,
balanced in the space
between the right brain lobe and the left.

It was indeed larger
than the door, to remove it
the thieves must have had
to disassemble it. It's a wonder
no one heard.

SIX AND A HALF WAYS OF LOOKING AT A CAT

(with apologies, of course, to Wallace Stevens)

I

Zen puss–
paw prints as
absences.

II

The eye of the cat is moving,
something must be flying.

III

Don't think of golden birds!
A metallic squawk,
then silence.

IV

The letters moved ecstatically
across the screen,
until a dark form leapt.

V

After dark all cats are gray
except this one,
the invisible.

VI

The cat likes poetry,
she preens herself
to the accents of Poe.

VI 1/2

An old woman and a cat are one.

THE THREE AGES OF EUROPE

Young she was an explorer
jumping nude into languages and oceans
sharing strange vehicles with stranger men
learning European words for hangover:
Katzenjammer, gueule de bois, resaca

Middle-age made of her a traveler
riding the metros without a map
sitting on concrete jetties
eating prosciutto and melon
dangling her feet in the Mediterranean

But now she's just a tourist
following the guide with red umbrella
who herds her along with other sheep
to the bus, or to the chosen bistro where
ready baguettes and coffees line the bar

EXTRACTIONS

four hours in the chair,
you rise bleeding,
teeth tiny bumps in the tray—

not the nightmare teeth
that gleamed at you from
corners of dream-rooms

but the bleak gray reality,
pain upon waking,
shaking hands and an unsteady floor.

thank you, you say so carefully
reaching for checkbook.
they will repair you later,

another day and repaint your face.
you feel violated.
small deaths, those bumps

like fetuses. you wish someone
would bring you soup, condole.
dizziness pushes your car

to the right, on the short
drive home. animals darting
into the brush look healthy,

toothy, feral. your house awaits.
you stare at mirrors. happy without reason,
you beam your Gothic smile.

THE CRONE AT THE CATHOLIC CONFERENCE

popcorn in a yellow machine with a red lid
I think of barrel-organs and monkeys

street dancers and tinny music
but this is a conference on the soul

in all the rooms left and right off this one
they are talking, talking, talking about the soul

the priests' and nuns' and brothers'
voices join in the hallway like old ghosts

the popcorn smells of butter
of old movies with Sydney Greenstreet

and Peter Lorre, its rich oily scent
slips under doors of conference rooms

where you are against Cartesian dualism
or you are not, are for it, you blind fool

long-ago summer afternoons gather
in shadows on the marquetry, under statues

the university is old, weathered, romantic
panes rattle in the sudden wind

outside fallen leaves whirl and drift
and we count, body, body, body, soul

ON THE GROUNDS OF THE MONASTERY WHERE FRA ANGELICO PAINTED

vietato entrare nel gardino

tree and dead plants,
sparse patches of grass
brick-lined paths from ancient arch to arch
anonymous weeds

ne pas entrer dans le jardin

cigarette butts
from scofflaws, maybe the groundskeeper
scraggly pansies, circle
of bricks around a barren tree trunk

der eintritt in den garten ist verboten

rusty pump off to the left
no songbirds would come here,
Eden stripped for the movers
pebbles mingle with dirt in tepid sunlight

do not enter into the garden

GALILEO'S EYE

In the Cafe of the Planets
    Galileo's eye
stares through centuries

the eye red-veined
    tired from seeing
wide under reddish lid

My own eyes weighted
    old and sleepy
Galileo looks at me

his truth hanging there
    opaque, not transparent
perpetually revolving

the abstract beauty of machines
    their gold gleam
an astrolabe tells the light

secrets he deciphered
    folding up again around
other centers

clutching
    other secrets
to their hearts

****

  boys swimming in a lake by a bridge

in a female season
shoulders touched by zephyrs

moon-drawings startling in their precision
the pencil tracing the phases
a language of symbols

so that 500 years later
an old woman gasps, says, yes that is it
that is the moon

****

"The Bible teaches how to go to heaven,
not how the heavens go"
he wrote to the Grand Duchess Christina.

Of course the Inquisition
stopped by,
sniffing for heresy,

and scenting it. Galileo's eye
did not wish to veil itself
or glance away, but he had to

look aside, askance
you cannot look the Inquisition
in the eye and live

he did not truly say
"but it still moves"
after the decree, though still it did

****

In Galileo's dream one daughter, the beautiful nun
who loves him whole-souledly, prays for him every day,

tells him at last the secret names of the numbers.

He knows it all, then, everything comes together
the way no one had ever even dreamed it,
the system, his understanding, a great clap of thunder.

****

Galileo was blinded by glaucoma,
not by looking at the sun
as was reported. The sun

did him no harm, nor did the moon and stars.

Grandmother guides grandson to the telescope,
shows him how to use it. He catches his breath
at the curve, the long unscrolling
of heaven.

OLD CINDERELLA

Arthritic fingers fasten the diamond tiara
(That glass slipper in a case, backlit)

Prince long gone in a drunken duel
Over someone's daughter

Never wanted another, took up sewing
But now can't make the tiny stitches

Invites Drusilla, remaining stepsister
To the castle for tea

(Castle is entailed and will go
To her son)

Dru a retired washerwoman
With red hands

Will snag a bauble for the pawnbroker
Though Cindy gives her money

Cindy tells her granddaughter
Marry a carpenter

SYLVIA AT SIXTY

After forty you don't think of knives,
they don't glitter seductively in drawers.
(Yesterday I cut my hand again,
an unexpected piece of sharp steel
when I tried to fix the fan. Blood dripped darkly
over the stilled blades. Only six stitches,
the Novocain hurt worst.)

She would have settled back into forms,
the blood-jet stilled, her craft fine-tuned by reading.
She would have always been the guest-lecturer
who was nervous, complained about the room
but gave a great speech.
She would have been read, but more like Donald Justice.

Her final housemate
would have been an airedale. She would have been most careful
about his health. Her children and grandchildren
would visit now and then, but not stay long.

Gardening, birds in the garden, grackles, sparrows,
jays and wrens. Purple marten feeder
above the sweetpeas, no more angry bees.
Daddy, old ghost,
can't call me now.
Anyway, I'll join you soon enough.

THE CRONE AT THE CATHEDRAL

Bell ringing violently
Huge bells jumping in the tower
Curves of metal scaring off the pigeons

And rain cuts the breath
As I kneel at wooden pew
Among dark-clad elders in first light

Mumble prayers in another language
And take the candle my neighbor
Gives you, hold it in my palm

The cylinder, the bright point of light
And I don't know what it is for
But desire is returning, though the church

Is cold, amidst the prayers
Of centuries, and the smell of old stone
And dust, and the statues

Worn shiny in places by touching,
And the incense, curl of gray smoke,
And desire, that dove in the belly, returning

LAUNDRY

So many clotheslines hanging in sun, rain
or snow, whites, blues, dingy along the tracks
or bright in fields, between tall buildings in cities,

reflecting the day's mood: grey, acid,
brilliant, inspired. I don't see anyone hang it up
but there it is, a statement, this is my life

for all to read. And now it is my turn,
with arthritic fingers I clip slips, sweaters,
shirts to the line. Will it freeze,

will the wind shatter it to ribbons?
A haphazard poet, I am careful with this,
my lines must be even, come to full stops.

Blouses in front, sweatshirts, heavy towels
in back, the damp fabric of them
weighing down the cord. I step away,

rub chilled, stiff hands, remember all the wearings,
smudges of work, of sweat, wrinkles and crumplings
erased now, look at the clean lines.

THE BOOKSTORE ON BROADWAY IN ALBANY: AWP CONFERENCE 1999

In the window, children's hardbacks
from the seventies, foxed spines,
ripped covers. Out front a rack
of faded fly-specked rain-spotted paperbacks.
It's almost dark in there, I make my way
among the racks and racks of crumbling
paperbacks, magazines, the precarious stacks
of books and music. Mouse dirt. Ants.
Dust over everything. At first the room
looks empty but then I spot an ancient
Irishman slumped on a rusty metal chair.
I find a Nero Wolfe for 35 cents
and give him two quarters. Once back
at the hotel, I stop to think,
maybe I missed a first edition Poe, or
a *Leaves of Grass* in there! So I return,
but the place is all closed up, a big
black padlock on the door. And I am glad,
for the long dark room was balanced at the point
between holding separate books and only dust
that would drift out through the city
in a sullen cloud, and finally disperse
to a tepid papery smell over Albany.
I should have known, passing over tinny quarters,
that our commerce took place there at the very edge,
that it was nightfall, that we were poised
between coherence and chaos,
between history and annihilation.

THE AUTUMN NAME OF GOD

Color, said the nun, is the autumn
name of God
and his winter name is Silence

and here is how it is for us:

we have only color and silence left
the leaves burn beautifully in their slow dying
the wind through the branches
makes a music like a lullaby
it carries back the names of other seasons

autumn is the last color of the house

framed there at the end of the path
amidst brilliant oaks and maples
we don't see its peeling paint,
the way the shutter hangs by a hinge

reds and yellows blow across the path,
pile up against the wall

soon, bare branches and snow

the coming of silence
God's final name

CASTIGLION FIORENTINO SATURDAY

Because I am missing a front tooth
and my dentist is 2000 miles away
I make friends with the person others call
the crazy catlady and who lacks
the same tooth. I sit next to her while she
feeds them; they come out of the bushes
around the bench. I have bought cat food too
but they won't come near me. I would
give my cat food to her but she says,
Just wait, put it out and wait. I do.
We sit and talk, *Have you been
doing this for a long time? Twenty
years or so, not long.* We converse
carefully because I have only got to
lesson five in the Italian book and it
doesn't really cover this situation, has more
to do with buying train tickets. Cats
(5 of them now) cluster around her feet,
eat up her food. *I have five of my own,*
she says, *my place is too small for any
more cats.* I know then she is not a crazy
catlady or she would have dozens. Her plate
is almost empty now, and finally
an orange longhair with bushy, matted
fur edges in my direction. Sniffs at the
plate. Digs in. And then all the others
join him, a ring of them, gobbling up
the pellets, conversing in cat,
which I understand at least as well as
I do Italian. Stunned with happiness,
I look at the catlady. She mirrors my smile.

MOVEMENT, SOLITUDE, SPACE

Waking with a cat
Next to you, is comfort—
She is not a threat or an obligation
And is complete in herself,
Has no need of you or
Anyone, though she is happy
With your company. She yawns languidly
And grooms herself. Perhaps you might like
To get up.

*

I know it is quite wrong
To let the water drip in the sink for the cat
But I do it sometimes
She gives a joyous leap
Into the bowl and I imagine
What it is for her:
A great hole in the sky
And the purest essence
Falling drop by drop before your nose
And you're thirsty

*

Cat people do not demand love
Or give it well, they are more used to
Wary friendship. A shared meal,
Your rights respected and mine, and the distance
Between us. There is the cold fresh call
Of the moon, starlight on the rough
Singled roof. The distance.

*

My best friend feared and
Hated cats. I had to lock them away
Before she came. Once one escaped
And she ran screaming. On TV
We saw the Tasmanian Devils on the nature channel.
They howled and bit each other and stripped
The land right down to the dirt. That is what cats
Are like, she said, underneath.

*

Sleep has withdrawn her webs,
Nothing between you and the night sky.
The window is open
And the planets wheel over you.
How temporary you are!

AT THE LIENDO

Hempstead, Texas, August 2004

Lunch at the grand old house turned restaurant,
wide porches, scrawled menu-slate,
flagstone walk, hedges and shrubs, wildflowers–

and a dozen cats and kittens on the porches,
snoozing in groups, nosing kibble, chasing
invisible insects over the varnished boards–

and we play with them, half tame, half feral,
letting us touch, but arched and poised to run,
until it's our turn to sit on bentwood chairs,

be fed etouffe and sweet tea, and talk
of past good times, while now and then at windows
a tiny face appears and vanishes.

I don't want to know what will happen after.
I want to think that life can just spread out
sometimes, sleepy and shiny, voluptuous,

cats, green jasmine, trumpet vine, mint.

SLEEPING WOMEN IN MOVIES

She is sprawled arms akimbo
   Yawns and stretches luxuriously
In black and white, tosses a satin pillow
Or she is curled on a lush divan
   Shrugs off the cat
           Reaches for her cell phone playing Bach
Or she wakens to a bird call, a slant of light
Rubs from her eyes the shreds of dream
Pads to the kitchen in her bunny slippers

Ah, to enact sleep,
Its accouterments,
Its ebbing tide
Your tresses spread over the bed's edge—
To fall asleep to, and to wake to, fiction—

THE CAT AT THE END OF THAT POETRY ANTHOLOGY

the striped cat is at the garbage pail
on the last page of the book
average cat, standard pail. his paw poking
a greasy paper bag of tin cans
and crumpled paper; you can smell
a rich sardiny smell of the seventies
wafting down the gray alley
where he's come
from mating and prowling
hungry

his delicate step certain
on all uneasy surfaces
mattress spring
hanging bird feeder
cyclone fence
window box
where they are planting grass
in sweaty summer bedrooms
sheets slick with pizza and love

Tom-of-the alley
archback surefoot
not afraid to touch

and oh, that beautiful rancid freedom

MONASTERY CATS

3, black and white,
gray, brindled, jump
to the kitchen window ledge
at San Lorenzo di Brindisi.

the hills around Rome are fading
and a single orange
falls from the tree
into the herb garden.

in a lighted square
a woman at the sink,
hair covered with
white restraining cap.

what is here is what
has always been here,
cloth, dishpan,
chalice, beaker, spoon,

matins, vespers. cats
rub against the window,
she puts the scraps out
in the last light,

from my borrowed cell
maybe a quarter mile away
I think I hear their purring,
her singing.

IN ANOTHER BAR

a bunch of drunks are laughing, celebrating
the great smashup of the Ten Commandments statue.
The wish they had it in video. It's gone from Facebook
and the ones on You-tube do not clearly show
the crash, the flying chunks of concrete,
the square-shaped space where it was, though they have
the shout of *Freedom!* and the sound of breakage.

I am drinking coffee, feeling unwelcome here, and
one of the drunks grabs my elbow. *Whaddaya think,
lady?* I am thinking I should have stopped
at the coffee shop but it was much too full.
But I respond that I don't support anyone's
smashing up anyone else's anything.
One of the drunks buys the old lady a beer.

Freedom! they all shout, *we all need Freedom,
even the old lady here.* I thank them,
pretend to sip, but somewhere the tiny
theologian in me is trying to figure it out—
when he hit the gas, lurching madly forward
and smashed all the Commandments to gritty chunks,
which, if any, did he actually break?

IN THE ALZHEIMER'S WARD

Well-lit, a giant colorful playpen,
bright fish in huge aquariums
and tropical birds in cages big as windows.

Old children in sit in wheelchairs
or on benches, one is curled up tight
in the beanbag chair, like a museum's

display of birth. A posted schedule
presumably for visitors and staff,
announces 3 *o'clock, memory.*

After the television hour, after nap,
well before dinner, they will have memory.
This is the best Alzheimer's ward

in the country, a visitor
murmurs. Before nap, after television,
daily, comes memory. On each door

a photo, *Doris, Eunice, Dora May
lives here,* photos like those on Italian gravestones.
A sweet-faced woman sits with an armful of shoes:

*They have forgotten them, I will keep them
for them, they leave them everywhere.* Another
pulls at blotchy arms, says *Look what they did to me.*

But most are silent. Still, at three o'clock
they will have memory. At three o'clock
the memory cheerleader will come dancing in.

Mother, she will say slowly, gesturing,
Father. Home. Husband. Wife. Children.
But surely, surely it is better not to remember,

to look at the bright wings, the sleek fish,
to hold the teddy bears sitting around on tables
(that belong to no one in this communist country)

and to watch the clock hands move? But the memory cheerleader
comes, she will lead them. *Husband, mother, home.*

THE CRONE AT THE AUSTIN POETRY FESTIVAL

patches of light and shade on the outside table
of the Austin café where this is happening

a train hooing in the middle of a line:
a caesura–a trembling voice picks up again

eyes closed, the crone still sees the flicker
of leaves blowing dark and light behind her lids

a sestina stops sharp at the end of every line
like a French chef is chopping it into segments

and she opens her eyes to a padlock and a screen
behind which other tables sit on an overgrown

lot, a café the mirror of this one, but abandoned
and silent, and she dreams herself gone over

beyond the screen, to the sunlit table
where now the 70s Austin poets she remembers

ghost the white chairs, David Yates, Jim Cody,
Joseph Colin Murphey; Susan Bright joins them

and they listen, smile and shake their heads
as if to say, that line is not quite right

but the *feel* of it is right, about the war
and hunger, the strange American lack of love

shadow-arms raise glasses of blue wine
to toast each other, and the crone wonders

when, what day, she'll find herself among them,
at those other tables, listening in full sun

OLD FRIENDSHIP

she's 30 and he's 50, they
meet in the hall outside his office
he's the hot new prof who used to be
a journalist, she's a mommy-track lecturer
*don't write a novel about the english
department*, he says, *everyone
does that*, and so
she doesn't

she's 40 and he's 60
they meet in a high alcove
of the library, drink forbidden coffee,
look down on antlike students, quote Shakespeare
about students, colleagues, she's tenure
track at last and his new book,
halfway between journalism
and scholarship, has hit
all the bookstores

she's 50 and he's 70
they meet at a gas station
on the edge of campus, he's newly
retired, she's newly promoted, they watch
people they know pass by on their
way to class, she wonders if he
has regrets, he says no but
she does not believe him

she's 60 and he's 80
they meet at McDonald's now
they discuss WWII, which he was in,

old movies and old wars in the classroom,
in the department, in the university
no one either knows passes by
he says *will you retire*
and she says *no*

she is 70 and he's 90
they still meet at McDonalds
sit on the same side of the table and discuss
their hemorrhoids and cataracts, decide
against surgery

THE GALLERY OF LOST ART

"Amber Room: dubbed the 'Eighth Wonder of the World,' the room that once symbolized peace was stolen by Nazis, then disappeared for good."

the gallery of lost art
belongs in itself, being
a member of its genre: the gallery
was never real, a digital display
taken down after a single year,
lost art re-lost, how can you re-lose
something unfound?

a child of five in a museum,
she read, carefully, *do not touch the art.*
she edged closer, wanting to touch,
just to feel the frame's edge. men in a boat,
thick blue paint strokes, the feel of rushing air.
she thought if her fingers grazed the frame
she would be there with them in the boat. a tall man
in a uniform approached, said *don't touch,*
but gently. so she didn't. she just looked.
seventy-odd years on she remembers that.

who made it, Manet? she will never know.
is it still in the museum, is the room
there still? but she has the art. untouched.

how, then is art lost?
     some destroyed by artist
     some destroyed by fire or flood
     some misplaced forever

      some stolen and never recovered
      some painted over
      some vandalized for materials
      some vandalized for fun
      some just a line in a letter: "Today I finished
the painting of Jean in the garden..."

an adolescent, she dreamed of finding the Amber Room.
she would wander into a woods in Germany
and go through a hole in an old stone wall
and there it would be, with the paintings, the statues,
a hundred shades of gold...

(the Russians reconstructed it from pictures,
but the new one looks like the photos,
not like the old one. no one knows the real one,
the one that's gone.)

an old woman, she knows art
is made to be lost. it is faded, fragile colors
of fleeting places, worlds that pass
even as the artist blends the colors.
and yet it concentrates the evanescent,
its beauty, its existence, sealed in time.

from WIDOWING

for Hugh McCann, 1942-2016. In all but fact, still with me.

Sleeping in your study I am assuaged,
The bedroom hurts. My own room
Has too hard surfaces
And the light comes too soon.

In your study under the San Damiano cross
Next to your old map of Ireland,
Near St. Thomas Aquinas and all the music
I will never listen to, though you tried.

Your awards are tucked away in corners
And in this room I sleep and dream and wake
Lulled by your scent
Cradled in your absence.

*

What will always bring you back:
Flowers in vases
Crossword puzzles
Sharpened pencils—he did the Sudoku and crossword with pencil
    leads like pinpoints.
Omelets—his were clouds, mine were doorstops.
New frying pans. We must have fifteen to twenty frying pans. I
    say we, but of course it is I who have these pans. What to do
    with them?
Beethoven and Mozart.
Sibelius and Strauss because he disliked them.
Arguments about God. Especially those I overhear but do not
    participate in.

Sports on tv but especially boring ones with a lot of green in
   the background.
Certain movies watched over and over, Fargo, A Perfect Murder,
   Far and Away, Ghost Busters—no real common denominator.
Stamp collecting gear.
Mass.
Stacks of quarters all ready for toll booths.
All the rites and rituals of Christmas, playful and serious,
   especially electric trains roaring around an old man's table.

*

You were the first face in the morning
And the last at night.
How many mornings and nights in fifty years?

I am looking at the last flowers you bought
Which outlasted the funeral flowers,
Though they are all withered now, and dropping petals.
in high school, walking along the rural road
headed for the ice-cream place
friends holding hands.
kid maybe ten on bicycle—
are you two in love?
we look at each other,
are we?

*

The word *widow* sounds like without. *Widower* more like
Something that you do.

*

your study in our second house
big as a garage,

giant chalkboard. you gave practice lectures
to the dog, the kids fled,
The center of the circles you drew
always said *God,*
the periphery changed with the seasons.

*

our best thing—Europe.
my parents sent us on our honeymoon,
your delight in everything, you who had never
even eaten steak until my mother served it.
cathedrals, art, the Salzburg music festival,
the glittering city, the water,
the Sommerhochschule were we supposedly learned
German, we read "Der Tonnel"
discussed it endlessly.

I think about it still, this silly guy in the tunnel
plunging toward, away from, in the dark,
his senses stopped by chosen obstacles,
the last line, "God as let us fall,
and we are rushing toward him."

These words came back to me when you were dying.
As comfort.

*

Sometimes it is as if

you left a glass of white wine
on the scarred end table,
rushing off to that airport

a full glass and I
straighten around it
vacuum beneath it

the lamplight hits it
a brighter center
glows like a candle flame

next day the sun shines through it
all the angles of the day
slant its shadows

lines and curves intersect
the cone of light grows
I sniff it

is it a cabernet
a sauvignon perhaps pinot grigio
a light dust has fallen on the table

any moment you will come home
see it, gulp it down
get back to work

TRIAGE

for my husband Hugh, 1942-2016

True, your father's sermons and the family
photos a great-grandchild might want,
but these holy cards with unfamiliar names—
grand-uncles and aunts of yours I never met—
cards with old devotions not practiced now—
faded, split, mildewed, spotted, ripped—

my hand hovers over the trash bin
wanting and not wanting to discard.
These belonged to your parents, grandparents,
and closing my eyes I see them, and you too,
a line of Irish faces growing smaller
into the past. I see you an altar boy,

dueling your brother with the torches
or pinching the communion wine (it wasn't
Christ's blood yet, so the only sin was theft—)
My hand falters. I can't keep these,
they are almost dust. The world I'm in
is difficult enough. Words flake off prayer cards.

I gather them up again, take them out
to the recycle box and put them in. I'm hoping
however they are reused, a molecule or so
of faith will still be there, that even as napkin,
paper cup, dictionary, notebook, cardboard box,
somehow the hand that touches it will sense

a subtle inspiration, gentle pull
toward something that I pray will be there still.

QUESTION POSED BY A PAINTING OF SAVONAROLA

"The world has come to such a state that one can no longer find anyone who does good."

—Girolamo Savonarola.

I always gave Savonarola short shrift—
"The mad monk who nearly
wrecked the Renaissance," they called him.
I have walked the pavement where
the Vanities burned, art works, mirrors,
lace tablecloths thrown into the flames
by impassioned young monks. And yet
he was a poet too, of burning heart,
promising to redeem Florence for God.

Talking of iniquity, he said, "It begins in Rome
where the clergy make mock of Christ and the saints;
yea, are worse than Turks and worse than Moors.
They traffic in the sacraments. They sell benefices
to the highest bidder. Have not the priests in Rome
courtesans and grooms and horses and dogs?
Have they not palaces full of tapestries and silks,
of perfumes and lackeys? Does it seem
that this is the Church of God?"

And now I'm back in Firenze,
way, way back. I hear the men approach,
heavy footsteps thud on paving stones.
They enter, tear my mother's jeweled combs,
right out of her hair, unwrap our silk scarves,

fill a box with my pictures of nymphs by streams.
Outside the shouts rise, flames make
a widening circle. We feel chastised
but not crushed; I'll give, I think,
my florins to the poor, I won't replace
my ribbons or my dresses. After all
no one is arresting us, and now
the men are going on to the next house.

They burned the monk where he had built his fires.
So if I see him rounding my corner now,
his black cloak flapping as he steps over kudzu,
broken brick and poison oak, a pile of dog poop,
should I lock the door or just invite him in?

MEMORY LANE

Beguiling little street in the museum,
cobblestones and 1940's drugstore,
plaster druggist with round shiny glasses.
Next door, massive TV's in windows.
Station One is broadcasting the news
and you can stand and speak there, to be seen
on the TV. At the telephone exchange
bright-nailed women, hair in victory rolls,
plug things in and tiny connections light.
Grandkids like the old technology, but find
the dentist scary, he doesn't have cartoons
on the walls or soothing music. I like him;
he looks like my old tormentor who gave me
comic books and lollipops when done.
I spend a lot of time explaining things
I don't know much about. Next, Dinosaurs.

*

In Holland there's a town that is a home—
a Memory Lane designed for Alzheimer's patients.
Time stopped for them a long time ago,
and now they just live in their past in peace.
Researchers don't know if it slows the progress
of the disease but the dwellers there are happy.
Of course there is a theory to the practice;
"Psychologist Donald Spence defines the concept
of 'narrative reality' as the ways in which
stories and places help link the 'true' world
to one that a person is able to understand . . . "
Hence all the stores and restaurants of the past,

the churches, bars, and groceries. No money,
all commerce is included in the fee.
Some relatives visit every day.

*

My friend the post-humanist tells me, "Soon
we'll have the handle on immortality,
we'll all be files on some immense computer,
living our lives in our favorite worlds
with our favorite people, we can do anything."
"And if your favorites have different favorites?"
I ask. "Well, that's the beauty of it, they aren't there.
In your file they are just as you desire them.
In their own files they make the worlds they want."
I say, "So it is all invention, and you're really
alone?" He says, "How could it matter, since
for all intents and purposes you aren't?
It's like the perfect *here*, but it's forever."

*

Of course that's what nostalgia really is,
just making up the past that never was.
Perhaps I should go back to the museum,
see the marquee with *Gaslight*—Bergman's
shining curls! Charles Boyer's iron face!
I'll hand the plaster druggist a silver dime,
take whatever he gives me.

IN DREAMS

In dreams I'm always packing up to leave,
apartment, house, office, city, country.
I have two suitcases and backpack stuffed
but far too much left over, papers, projects

and shoes. I try to hide what I can't pack,
the room must be left clean. I shove things
into closets, under rugs, but my belongings
slip out of drawers. Laddered stockings,

panties with gone elastic, that loved shirt
I spilled paint on, the multiplication tables,
my old Bonneville, a black-browed sullen
boyfriend, the evil dentist, half a dozen cherubs

who emanate from slammed drawers like vapors,
two-headed rats I herd into the hall,
Poe, Anna Karenina and the Bible,
which, come to think of it, I ought to take.

THE CRONE RESPONDS TO A POEM ON VERSE DAILY WHICH COMPLAINS ABOUT USELESS POETRY THAT DOES NOT ADDRESS INJUSTICE

Would you rather read about
human trafficking or sunrise?

Sunrise, please. Horrors abound
and we did them. Still the sun comes up.

This morning I hobbled out toward the pink striae of sky
with my old dog, arthritic too.

We walked though a great spiderweb, did not flinch,
though sticky invisible threads covered our faces.

It was as though the world
was trying to keep us in it.

GUILT

Her hands are leaf-veined, lines
run down her fingers, maybe she's an oak.
If she stands very still.

Confess the tiny sins, the big ones
in the back of the closet grow.
The little ones march past the priest
in mary janes and pinafores, the big ones
exhale must and fetid air,
elbow each other for room.

She can't even name them.
she calls a bad word into the closet,
something snuffles and huffs but stays inside.

*I'm not sure if someone hit my car
or I hit someone's. My son says
better to be the hitter than the hit.
I say not so, if I hit someone
I feel guilt, if he hit me, anger.
I'd rather feel anger than guilt.*

Pure anger is best,
for the injustices of everyone.
Hard to get there though. Crackling ire
is usually personal, not noble.

She loved the sun's eclipse for the dancing
crescents of light on the fallen leaves,
not for the dark.

Wallace Stevens said oak leaves
are hands. Are not hands oak leaves?
Do they draw power from blood or sap?
She stretches hers out before her, empty,
for the gift of absolution, to hold it.

CROSSWORD

First clue I know right off—
"Dwight's competitor." I write ADLAI
and mother resurfaces, angry: "How can we
beat 'I Like Ike'? 'I'm madly
for Adlai'? We'll lose." And we did.
I have her button somewhere, all it says
is 'Adlai Stevenson.' Other clues
fall into place, some bringing images,
some not. I am supposed to do this,
the doctor suggested, for my mind,
that the syllables may not
slide down the fading roundnesses of brain,
collect in the dark skull
between the hemispheres.

But you really do it for your soul. You want
the secret message, from the Puzzler
to you alone, the hidden word
spelled diagonally or hidden otherwise.
After the Andrea Doria, and
the poor dog abandoned in space,
triumphs and tragedies and trivialities,
and what the hell is a kep?
You want to be in it, then, a part of the puzzle.
Your own name. Evoked, included.
When it's all filled in.

IN THE FRONT GARDEN

Solitude: the iron chair, the table.
Leaves drift down as I write.
The rake upended, the watering can
overturned, the hose an untidy curl.

Jasmine and pittosporum
and weeds that grow uninvited,
rusty clippers, a two-step ladder,
empty flower pots, one broken.

This November day, the 1280th
of my widowhood. You clipped bushes,
mowed back jasmine. I see you
now, taking the empty chair.

You don't accuse me of neglect,
point out the rubbish. You are just there.
The leaves fall to the table.
Perhaps tomorrow I will tidy up.

WALKERS OF THE SEEN AND UNSEEN

The man walks his dog, iconic.
The shepherd at his side lopes along.
A brief command, dog stops short,
looks at us. Now they cross the street
side by side, reflecting each other's rhythms.

But the old lady walking her poem, she's
different. It dodges across the street,
knocks over a garbage pail, takes off
with a package of expired bologna. She
whistles for it, curses, shakes a fist.
She can hear it, it's just out of sight.

The man walking his dog comes to the end
of another block, turns back, and sees
the poem lady with red face, scrunched eyes,
breathing fast and looking all around.
He does not say hello nor does he notice
her trailing leash, the rustling in the woods.

75TH 4TH

I think about the town fireworks
but stay home. Then I find a box of them
in my son's room—pieces 25 years old,
some of them powdery, some only wilted.

The biggest one is a tall cylinder
covered with cautions: **Stand back!
Do not relight! Never lean over the
tube!** So of course for my 75th 4th

I set it on my driveway and I light it,
expecting nothing. But a giant hiss
is followed by a hundred colored
balls of fire, then shooting stars

dart 30 feet into the heavens! I am
terrified, backed up against the wall.
My yard smells explosive, there's smoke
all over, a few last sparks die

on the pavement. I go inside, change
my nighty for a denim dress, and sit
at the window, waiting for the cops.
I hope they come.

CORONA

A friend who has cancer tells me
she has learned to live with ambiguity.
I haven't. I watch the virus spread,
black circles across the map coalescing.
Uncertainty was never my room of choice.
I always wanted to *know*. I want to think,
four weeks and it will be over. Six weeks tops.
Then everybody will get back to work.
Acquaintances will kiss.
The neighbor who never liked me and I
will hug, while our dogs, having forgotten
their lifelong enmity, will sniff each other.
The priest will offer the chalice at mass again.
We can share ice cream cones,
even with the dogs. My hands are shiny with washing.
They yearn for other hands, for the touch of skin.

CORONA BOREDOM

Must be a sin. Is. *I accuse myself
Of boredom.* Sloth? Not really,
Or not only. You can be bored
Mopping a floor, paying bills, even
Playing a game. *Your move!*
Ah, whatever.

A lack of connection, of connectivity.
No one else in the room. Your mind
Slides over the surfaces, not catching
On anything. *Mea culpa.*
But what did you do?
Nothing.

Ennui, but that is French boredom,
More interesting and sometimes quite active.
Implies inevitability, resignation.
*Helas, I have looked at the Seine
So many times from this very same perspective
It ceases to move me.*

No inner resources, said Berryman,
Bored beyond hope. What might they be,
Inner resources? A well at the back of the mind,
A vessel that never empties, but is hard
To find, requires for every thirst
A different route?

I have tried this tiresome path too many times.
Will start again, this time I'll turn left
At the tree.

ORDINARY TIME

"this is the first sunday
of ordinary time." i liked the priest's
announcement, it sounded like a prayer.

so many years i wanted celebration,
but now this is my desire:
no fast, no feast, just the gleam

of the chalice, the paten, with
the repeated words, the reassurance
that time is ordinary. nothing in particular

is going to happen. the sermon though
describes the wedding at Cana, which is
of course a feast, and some of that story

diffuses through the air like a promise.
i breathe deeper, look at the stained-glass window
of Jesus and wine jugs, and hope only

for more ordinary Sundays unfolding
one after another at ritual pace,
towards the unimaginable feast.

HOUSES

Nancy and I found a derelict house
in the middle of nowhere. Mostly empty rooms.
Wooden knickknack shelf,
moon-shaped, high on the wall.
Rusty pots and pans, a moldy couch.
Outside blackberries, poison oak, buckthorn,
no road. We played there afternoons
all summer, served cookies and blackberries
on the old pans, until my mother
found out somehow and made us stop.
Anyway it was time for school again.

Nancy and I hooked school
to go back one more time.
Our parents had scared us with stories
of murderous hobos in the woods.
There were none, but we
felt guilty for using the ghosts' things.

Nancy and I did not belong there,
We were trespassers. Forgive us.

#

We are not allowed to mourn the past,
It is not ours.

#

In *Ghosts along the Mississippi*, Clarence John Laughlin
caught with his lens the great decaying mansions,
walls fallen away, sons gone to the Civil War
or yellow fever (this French-style plantation house
built for a child who died at seven),
arms from broken statues
signaling warning and memorial.

The buildings will crumble into the river.
Some have.
A few are still lived in,
just a few rooms where the last of
the diminished family camps.

A poet-photographer friend
hunts for abandoned houses throughout Texas
and Louisiana, there are many.
She brings "her girls," nineteenth-century dresses
of silk, velvet, satin, lace. Drapes them
on torn divans, rotting windowsills,
their vivid colors sprightly against ruin.
A past erased but always present.

#

Those ghost-ridden mansions
on tv shows. Curving stairwells, statuary,
oil portraits of ancestors, echoes of
long ago passions, forgotten sins.

In these stories the house always wins,
and in the last scene the realtor is showing it to new
prospective buyers, not mentioning of course
the bodies in the basement, the vanishings.

The ancestors in the pictures
hold tenancy forever. "Old sins have long shadows."

And the thin, bitter film-maker explains:
*I halfway believe in my vision.
If there is any kind of afterlife
it must be this. Deformed, misshapen.
Nothing but a disembodied feeling.*

End of the long, long narrative:
—*Did you like it?*
—*I'm not sure. What actually happened?*
—*Did they die, or not?*

#

Possess. Possession.
I have three dolls, wrote the first-grader
Carefully on the line.
In *The Turn of the Screw*
Miles dies because he is dispossessed,
not for any other reason.

#

In dreams grandmother calls to me
from her rotted porch.
A bird (magpie?) flies across the sundial.
It was so dark in the living room, but now
Sunlight beams through broken slats
on revealed floorboards.
Grandmother shakes crumbs from her apron
for nineteenth-century birds.

For us exiles too: a whisper of mint in the wind.
Abandoned roses still crawling up walls.
Wallpaper of horses and carriages.
The two-button light switch, that of course
gave forth no light.

On the internet I looked up the spot
where my grandparents' house had stood.
The place where I watched the garage blow down
In the great New Jersey storm, from the safety of my crib.
Metal bars and framework crashed
against the house, which whined and shuddered.
But even the place where it was is gone.
Now there's a chi-chi street of boutique restaurants.

Some shade of us remains.
Ghost houses keep their inhabitants,
living and dead.

Somewhere my grandmother must be serving tea
from the silver pot and tray I have right here
in the glass cabinet. It's black as pitch.
No one has polished it for fifty years.

A house is a sentience
that death does not efface.

What we want:
to keep the past
behind a locked door, but there.
There.

MY GRANDDAUGHTER POSTPONES HER WEDDING BECAUSE OF THE PANDEMIC

The unspoken wedding gown is love.
Hanging in wait,
    moving its empty sleeves
on the invisible draft, it repeats the story
       of ritual and memory. Its silks whisper,
don't forget. don't forget.
          think of me if you can.
Outside there is a sheen on the air
    and flakes, like radiation, falling.
Everything, the world, waits.
From her front door the land spreads out its promise.

LIFE LIST

in memory of S. L. A.

My friend the scholar-birdwatcher
is dying, after a quiet regular life
of Milton and birds, and if I could

imagine him a farewell, it would be this:
to look out into the small yard
he tended for forty years, to where

he placed the bird houses, the martin
house and the hummingbird feeder,
just in time to see a sweep of air

curve in and take form, the great arctic gyrfalcon
not on his life list, there on the sill,
to be recognized by beak, feathers and pinions

and final knowledge, Adam's homecoming
after the story's end, better than Eden.
May he have in his hand a feather, that his wife

might know where he has gone.

NIGHT

Da, wo die graue, die Taube, aufpickt die Namen
diesseits und jenseits des Sterbens: (Paul Celan)

*There where the gray one, the dove, pecks up the names
this side and that side of dying...*

***

About the author

JOURNALS PUBLISHING JANET MCCANN'S work include *Kansas Quarterly, Parnassus, Nimrod, Sou'wester, America, Christian Century, Christianity and Literature, New York Quarterly, Tendril,* and others. A 1989 NEA Creative Writing Fellowship winner in poetry, Janet taught at Texas A & M University from 1969 until 2015, is now Professor Emerita. She has co-edited anthologies with David Craig, *Odd Angles of Heaven* (Shaw, 1994), *Place of Passage* (story line, 2000), and *Poems of Francis And* Clare (St. Anthony Messenger, 2004). She has written four poetry books and six chapbooks. Her most recent poetry book is *The Crone at The Casino* (Lamar University Press, 2014). She also has co-authored two textbooks and written a book on Wallace Stevens (*Wallace Stevens: The Celestial Possible,* Twayne, 1996). She is a Catholic, and she lives in College Station, Texas.

www.ingramcontent.com/pod-product-compliance
Lightning Source LLC
Chambersburg PA
CBHW051051160426
43193CB00010B/1143